The Daftest Rabbit Hops Again!
& other stories

DC THOMSON
MEDIA

Illustrations: Mandy Dixon
Images: Istockphoto, Shutterstock
Published in Great Britain by D C Thomson & Co. Ltd.,
185 Fleet Street, London EC4A 2HS.
www.dcthomson.co.uk

The Daftest Rabbit Hops Again!
& other stories

More stories about Ted, a rabbit of very little brain, who lollops through life wondering what on earth's going on and taking frequent naps to think about it, and his owner, who frequently finds himself in the same bewildered state but with less time available for napping. Enjoy a chuckle with this latest collection of Chris Pascoe's columns from My Weekly.

CONTENTS

The Daftest Rabbit Hops Again!

Animal Crackers

Chris Pascoe Collection 3

Epic Failures

Meet The Pets

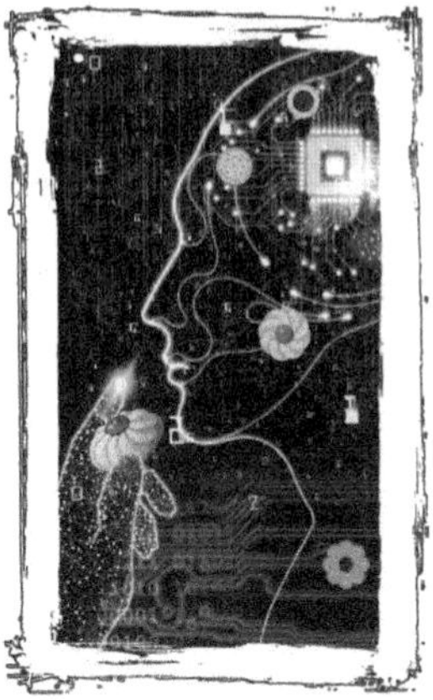

Fancy That

Chris Pascoe's Fun Tales

PUNCTUATION FRUSTRATION!

What was Chris trying to tell himself... and does Ted need to be afraid?

This morning, I opened my emails and stared at the message I'd sent myself the night before. It simply said, "Don't look up, rabbit".

Regular readers may remember I have a habit of waking in the night, grabbing my mobile phone and sending myself "important" messages... messages that occasionally prove useful, but more often than not are complete gobbledygook.

This definitely fell into the latter category. Was it a warning or a threat? →

It sounded as if, in a sleepwalking state, I'd been pointing a water-pistol at my rabbit Ted. But if that really was the case, knowing myself as I do, I'd have taken the opportunity to deliver the sentence in Elmer Fudd style, so my shout would surely have been "Don't look up, wabbit!" Not rabbit.

So, nope, I was barking up the wrong tree with that – and also with the idea that Ted's hyper-intelligent – but remember, I was dreaming.

After some time, I suddenly remembered what half-asleep me had been trying to tell me. The confusion lay with the comma – it shouldn't have been there.

I'd woken in a state of irrational excitement, thinking about My Weekly's book of my columns named *The World's Daftest*

It sounded as if, in a sleepwalking state, I'd been pointing a water-pistol at Ted?

Rabbit, and wondering if there had ever been a book in the history of the world all about a rabbit.

I immediately went on the internet for information, and got hit with a deluge of results that had me instinctively hiding my phone screen in case my wife woke up.

Hence, my hastily written reminder basically meant, when researching rabbits, "don't look up rabbit". Searching for "bunny" doesn't improve the situation either.

Anyway, I now recall drifting back to sleep answering my original question, "Peter Rabbit... Brer Rabbit... Miffy...Watership Down..."

OK, so that note wasn't going to be of much use on the column front. I skimmed down my emails and found another me-message. "Toilet Dalek!" shouted the subject line. I decided not to open it.

Of course, my night-note-to-self wasn't the first time a single comma has completely messed up a sentence, and the famous book title *Eats, Shoots and Leaves* points this out particularly well.

But my favourite ever error, in our local press, was an advert for a video rental shop (you can tell how far back we're going here) and involves not the misplacing of a comma, but of the entire advert.

If you're going to accidentally place any business address under a banner headline intended for a builders' merchants yard stating WE HAVE MOUNDS OF HARDCORE… it would probably be better if it wasn't for the village video shop!

THE GREAT ESCAPE

There's no place like home... especially with a pack of warring pets

Our two lapin friends, the World's Daftest Rabbit Ted and his feisty live-in-partner-girl-rabbit Billie, have been gradually edging their way into our house of late. They started with a hutch, progressed to a shed, made their way into warm indoor accommodation in our utility room, and this week, finally, overran the house.

The week began with my wife Lorraine buying a pop-up fabric playpen that covers the whole lounge floor, allowing them a daily change of scenery and a chance to stretch those great thumping back legs. The playpen came with a guarantee that within its sturdy frame and heavy duty fabric covering they'd be totally safe from predators (ie. Bodmin the cat).

But could the playpen stand up to Billie the rabbit and her

> Jojo came face to face with... horror of horrors... a dozy, lop-eared rabbit

giant gnawing buck-teeth? No, apparently it couldn't. I'd left the rabbits happily munching hay and staring at walls – standard rabbit stuff – and gone to get some work done on my computer (mainly watching videos of cats falling over) when I had the strange sensation that somebody was behind me.

Bodmin was out, and our two other cats, Spooky and her sister →

Jojo, were sleeping on a chair in front of me... so who was behind me? Slowly, tentatively, I looked over my shoulder, and there, sitting in the doorway was Ted, staring steadfastly at the back of my chair. A few feet behind him was Billie, jumping on a pile of rapidly disintegrating pampas grass she'd wrenched from a vase.

It took me a few seconds to comprehend what I was looking at. How, and why, were the rabbits in the hall? While I sat thinking about this, total mayhem suddenly broke out all around me. Alerted by Billie's jumping, Spooky woke in surprise and, as panicking cats tend to do, hissed and randomly smacked the innocently sleeping Jojo round the face. Jojo reacted with equal surprise, jumping up in fright and running full speed for the office door, only to come face to face with...horror of horrors...a dozy, lop-eared rabbit.

Jojo really hadn't been expecting this, and turned in alarm just in time to intercept an advancing Spooky, who now received a reciprocal paw swipe to the head. Ted meanwhile, hadn't moved a muscle. I'm not sure he even noticed the two screeching cats exchanging blows right under his idly twitching nose. He still didn't move when they locked in combat and rolled straight past him.

Billie did though, and performed a marvellously eloquent jump clean over the cats and onto Ted's back. He still didn't notice. The next few minutes would've been best accompanied by the Benny Hill theme tune, with me chasing in and out of rooms after Billie, criss-crossing running cats and narrowly avoiding the motionless Ted. It was just a very good job Bodmin was out attacking other things, like large dogs, and wasn't home to join in. After the storm came the calm, albeit leaving the devastation of a holed-playpen and destroyed pampas.

A home isn't a home without pets they say. Though it does at least stay in one piece.

HEAD, ELBOWS, KNEES & TOES...

With Chris's gross motor skills impaired, one accident leads to another

I've been a bit in the wars just lately. Stepping out of my car into a puddle that turned out to be just short of a small pond, I stumbled and splashed for around three yards before dropping heavily onto one knee.

So hard was the resulting knock, I remained motionless for a few moments, hands clasped in front of my face, almost up to my waist in water. Anybody watching may have mistaken me for trying to impersonate John the Baptist.

As I left the shop, my knee gave way slightly and I stumbled down the kerb

Luckily, as I do this sort of thing quite a lot, I already own a sports knee-support, so brought it back into use. The very next day I twisted my elbow driving, decided my elbow was worse than my knee, and put my knee support on my elbow.

Knee supports don't work brilliantly on elbows, making arm movements strange and jerky, and I first discovered this sitting at a set of traffic lights. Using the stationary moment to grab a Polo mint, I attempted to put it in my mouth and punched myself straight in the face.

Stunned at how hard I'd just hit myself, and unable to →

FISH CHIPS
fish & chips
TAKE-A-WAYS
HAMBURGERS

understand how, I brought my hand up again, experimentally, and smacked myself in the mouth.

At this point I noticed a man staring at me aghast from an adjacent car – he'd just spotted a man sitting at traffic lights repeatedly punching himself.

So, now feeling a bit battered and bruised, with a split lip, swollen knee and wearing a knee support on my elbow, I decided to console myself with some good old junk food. I hobbled into a fish 'n' chip shop and ordered a battered sausage, and I suppose, essentially, this was exactly what I was.

The server looked me up and down, shook his head, and scooped a free portion of chips in with the sausage. Great, he'd taken one look at me and thought I was homeless. I thanked him profusely though, realising as I did so that my lip was causing me to slur quite heavily, as if three sheets to the wind. I'd really pulled off a great look here, hadn't I?

As I left the shop, my knee gave way slightly, probably because I was wearing its support on the wrong limb, and I stumbled down the kerb, only managing to prevent another fall by clinging to a lamppost. I couldn't face looking back to see if the chip shop owner was watching.

I'm not the only one in the family with a propensity for accidental self-harming. No, the world's daftest rabbit, Ted, has recently been refusing to accept the existence of doors.

He's always had problems with doors, but just lately he's failing to understand the need to open them before going through them.

It's not only doors either. In fact, it seems that anything that can be opened but isn't open when Ted reaches it will be systematically head-butted. This has led to a number of situations recently. More on that next time.

BANG

CRASH, BANG, WALLOP!

Chris now has huge sympathy with Ted the rabbit's issue with doors...

I mentioned in my last column that Ted, my barely sentient pet rabbit – and so daft he's already featuring in his own book – has run into some new problems...doors. Literally. Ted has recently decided that doors don't exist, and is refusing to accept the need to open them.

This had always been a slight problem of Ted's. He's walked into doors before, but it's now become a daily thing. Ted seems to reason that if the doorway to his hutch was once open, it's always open, despite the evidence of a latched wooden door. He'll therefore walk towards it, getting closer and closer with no sign of slowing down as he reaches it, and then – bang! – walk headfirst into it and bounce backwards onto his bobtail.

He'll then sit staring at the door in total disbelief for a good

> Ted, The World's Daftest Rabbit, has always had a big problems with doors

ten minutes. His live-in-partner-girl-rabbit Billie generally looks up briefly, twitches her nose in contempt, and then goes back to munching hay.

It's not only doors Ted doesn't believe in – it's absolutely anything that opens and shuts. Ted believes that anything that was once open will always be open and that's final. →

This is particularly a problem with his timer-feeder. In an effort to regulate Ted's eating while we're out (i.e. prevent him from eating a day's worth of food in 20 seconds flat and then fainting) we purchased a clever little pet-feeder with multiple covered food trays that open at set times of the day. You've already guessed the problem here, haven't you? While Billie's already worked out how it all works, Ted of course has no idea whatsoever how it works and simply sits stubbing his snout on the container lids like one of those perpetual motion novelty toy birds repeatedly dipping its head into a bowl of water.

Another open-able rabbit door, the wire grill door of their run, is also seeing quite a lot of Ted lately. As with the hutch door, Ted attempts to pass through it in spirit-like fashion, only to be thwarted at every attempt. Only his nose, an eye and occasionally a lop-ear will get through, the rest of him remaining bunched up behind the wire.

After writing the above, I have to admit I've just proved once and for all that Ted may be dumb – but no dumber than his owner.

We've recently had new doors fitted. The difference between these doors and our old ones is that you need to turn the handle to open them, instead of just pushing the door. And so it was that I got up from my desk, holding my cup of coffee, and walked briskly to the office door, gave it a firm shove… and walked straight into it. I then returned to my desk covered in coffee and added this paragraph. And right there's a little insight to exactly how I work.

We share a lot of traits, Ted and I. "Barely sentient" being one of them…

MANNERS MAKETH THE RABBIT

Bumbling bunny Ted certainly has an unusual way with the ladies

Just lately, I've become increasingly concerned about the lack of manners being displayed around our household. I suppose that, with a teenage daughter in the house, bad manners could reasonably be expected and she certainly has a turn of phrase that's anything but polite – but she's not actually the worst offender.

No, that honour goes to a certain lop-eared rabbit of (in the words of AA Milne) very little brain. I refer of course to Ted – officially The World's Daftest Rabbit after being immortalised in a book of that name (something I'm sure he appreciates). Ted's manners around his long suffering live-in-partner-girl-rabbit Billie are, with no exaggeration, appalling. While Billie is prone to bouts of sudden violence, her treatment of Ted is predominantly very good. She washes and grooms him for hours on end, and

> On closer inspection, I realised the ridiculous truth – Ted was biting his own toenails

sometimes he even notices she's doing it. Is Ted grateful? No, not at all – as time's gone by, he's become less and less likely to ever return the pampering compliment.

It was a big surprise then when, the other day, I noticed Ted vigorously washing the top of Billie's head for quite a considerable length of time. However, on closer inspection, I realised the ridiculous truth. While it looked for all the world as though he →

Nibble
Nibble
Ping

was washing her, he actually had his foot on her head and was nibbling at his own back claws. So, in effect, he was using Billie's head as a prop so he could bite his toenails. That's nice, isn't it? I can't actually imagine worse manners.

To make matters worse, when he'd finished dealing with his feet, he suddenly jumped on her back in what must have been his thousandth unsuccessful attempt to mount her. Can there have been any worse come-on in history than first chewing your own toenails?

The main cause of failure in Ted's latest half-hearted mating attempt was that it took place on the very top shelf of their hutch, much too close to the roof. There really isn't room for double-decker rabbits on that shelf and, predictably, Ted got wedged between Billie and the ceiling. His frantic attempts to then escape involved pushing forward and down over Billie's face.

An increasingly annoyed Billie waited patiently while her cumbersome partner untangled himself, then took two steps forward and delivered a vicious back-kick to his ears, causing him to reach the lower levels of the hutch far faster than he'd planned. For Ted, all this was situation normal and after taking a few seconds to compose himself, he started munching on the pile of hay he'd landed in.

Incidentally, on the subject of manners, I heard a song by a band named Bad Manners the other day, called *Lorraine*. Now, while my wife Lorraine hasn't yet been mentioned in this column due to her usually impeccable manners, this song contained the lyrics *Lorraine's a flipping con* and more worryingly *Lorraine punched me on the nose*. Not such good manners after all then, Lorraine?

A DAY OF FURRY FURY

What happens when a radicalised rabbit goes rogue? Dodge those pellets!

Though being of sound mind, my wife Lorraine has long been convinced our rabbits enjoy listening to the radio. Is that really a rabbit thing? When we walk through meadows, do we ever hear the strains of Radio 2 echoing from burrows, scores of pointy-eared nose-twitchers humming along to Jive Bunny? No we don't. And Lorraine doesn't even play music stations for our rabbits, Billie and Ted, as she thinks they benefit more from talk radio – rabbits as they do, having no interest in politics whatsoever.

While listening to the issues of the day from their utility room multi-storey cage seems to have no effect on our out-of-it full time hay muncher Ted, his partner rabbit Billie does seem to nibble far more urgently on her carrots whenever debates become heated – Brexit has cost us a fortune in mixed veg. In fact, I feel all those radio "calls to action" have really appealed to Billie, so it's highly possible the BBC have radicalised our rabbit.

So much so that, last Tuesday, she staged her very own Day of Fury. That morning, from the moment Billie woke Ted by jumping three feet onto his back and sending him crashing sideways off his straw bed, we could tell she was in feisty mood. Ted looked vaguely surprised but nothing much bothers him, not even Days of Fury. Lorraine was very much bothered though, when five minutes later, Billie bit her. Now, while Lorraine believes this to have been down to slightly short-sighted Billie mistaking her finger for a →

carrot, I really can't go along with this – okay, Lorraine's tanning moisturiser might be a bit over-effective at times, but she's never aspired to bright orange, so I just can't accept Billie thought she was a carrot. To me, this was just another escalation of Billie Fury (just to be clear here, Billie Fury is now the official title of Billie's rabbit rebellion, and I attach no blame for the biting of Lorraine's finger to 1960s rock'n'roll star Billy Fury).

Worse was yet to come. Upon release into their bad-weather indoor play pen, Billie paced and cased the area like an inmate in a US prison exercise yard. Something was afoot, and with the size of Billie's back feet, it was going to be big. Suddenly, it all kicked off, literally – Billie back-kicked her water bowl across the pen, sending water splashing through its fabric-mesh walls, far enough to spray

Billie then picked up a paper plate in her mouth and slapped Ted in the face with it

a sleeping cat on a nearby armchair (luckily not bruiser tomcat Bodmin, or things really would have kicked off).

Next, and without a pause for breath, she picked up a paper plate in her mouth and slapped Ted in the face with it, rabbit pellets flying in all directions. With Ted wondering what hit him, Billie raced to the edge of the pen, reached a gnawed hole she'd been working on for weeks, ripped it open with two buck-teeth and hopped through onto the lounge carpet. She'd escaped. It all ended with Billie getting kettled (though without the need for riot shields) and taken back to the safety of her cage via cat-carrier transport. The Day of Furry Fury was over.

ANOTHER FINE MESS...

Chris contemplates how Billie and Ted could be named Stan and Ollie

Writing my column a couple of weeks back, all about Billie and Ted, the slightly dysfunctional rabbit community of our wholly dysfunctional household, I suddenly realised just how much they resembled one of my all time favourite comedy duos, Laurel and Hardy. Not in looks you understand – I've never really looked at Stan and Ollie and immediately thought 'RABBITS', but very much so in personalities and ways.

Having said that, Ted's wild hairstyle is vaguely reminiscent of Stan Laurel's, but it's the big lop ears that give it away (Ted's...not Stan's). It's Ted, of course, who's Laurel – dopey, loveable, accident prone, and overall, not quite with it, while Billie's a definite Hardy – long-suffering, generally exasperated, quick tempered and prone to sudden acts of retaliatory violence. They're a perfect match!

But, it's their actions that really cement the deal. I watched a Laurel and Hardy clip the other day, in which the pair attempt to sweep a chimney. It was almost like watching Ted and Billie on any given day of their lives! Firstly, with Ollie stationed on the roof, Stan's brush suddenly shoots out of the chimney, hitting Ollie square in the face, along with about a ton of soot, and sending him sprawling off the roof and straight through a shed below, totally collapsing it. If this isn't Ted's regular habit of flinging all his bedding hay into Billie's face as she pokes her nose into their sleeping compartment, generally sending her toppling back down →

her ladder into a litter tray, I don't know what is! It even creates as much of a dust explosion as Stan's soot!

On climbing back onto the roof, shaken and blackened from head to toe, Ollie then sits down on a roof skylight window, only for Stan to hurl it open from indoors, propelling Ollie back into the wreckage of the shed like a rocket. This is more or less exactly what happens whenever Ted tries to use the rabbit pen's catflap-style door. He's never once been able to get through the thing without landing in a heap the other side, but what he does manage to do, when attempting to follow Billie through, is swing it wildly open with an exploratory headbutt. This results in Billie, who's had no time at all to get clear of the door, receiving a sudden smack to the backside that sends her sprawling across the sawdust floor at high speed. Of course, whenever any of these incidents occur – just as a furious Ollie retaliated in the clip by covering Stan so liberally in soot it was hard to discern which was the chimney sweep's brush and which was Stan (especially with that haircut) – an absolutely livid Billie does very much the same sort of thing, back-kicking so much hay and sawdust in Ted's direction you lose sight of him for a while.

It's Ted, of course, who's Laurel – dopey, loveable, accident prone and not quite with it

So there you have it. Stan and Ollie are alive and well, and currently residing in a High Wycombe rabbit hutch!

Chris Pascoe's Fun Tales

TED'S COTTAGE CALAMITY

Taking other people's advice never seems to work out well in Chris's world

I read a newspaper report recently, relating to a man who was attacked by a bear and managed, after a struggle witnessed by his girlfriend, to fend it off. Somehow though, the newspaper report managed to present the incident in a very different way… as if the bear was actually retaliating: a man survived being mauled by a 6ft brown bear which savaged his leg after he punched it in the face on the advice of his girlfriend.

This actually makes it sounds very like a confrontation in a dubious late night inner-city pub… "Dave, that big brown bear at

> *Ted sat in the corner and watched, astonished, as Billie began eating the cottage*

the bar's been staring at me all night and giving me really nasty looks." "Which one, Tracy?" "The bear! I reckon he fancies me Dave… in a 'nasty looks' sort of way." Dave looks long and hard at the colossal mass of muscle and iron claws standing growling at the bar. "Well, what exactly do you want me to do, Tracy? He's a giant bear!" "Just punch him in the face, Dave!" And then, inevitably… "Arghhhh, my leg, my leg, ARGHHHHH!"

Someone else taking poor life advice from his girlfriend this week – or at least following her ways – has been my rabbit Ted (now officially immortalised as The World's Daftest Rabbit in a →

munch
munch
munch
munch
munch
munch

book of the same name). Ted likes the simple life which, with his general understanding of everything, is just as well.

So on the rare occasions he wakes up, he tends to look to his live-in-partner-girl-rabbit Billie for guidance. Thus was the case when I brought them home a treat described as a Carrot Cottage. This magnificent thing is a rabbit sized house, complete with four walls, a door and a roof, and made entirely from carrots. Ted totally misunderstood the purpose of his new edible home, and instead of eating it, or even sitting inside it, tried to hump it.

There are certain lines Billie will not tolerate being crossed with regard to food, and this was one of them. A brief fight ensued, which Billie obviously won, leaving Ted sitting in a corner, nose twitching, watching in astonishment as Billie began eating the cottage. As he began to comprehend exactly what was happening, his ears pricked up in delight, and with two giant rabbit bounds, he hopped onto the roof of Carrot Cottage and began happily munching away.

The big difference in the pair's approach of course, was that Billie was eating the base of the house, Ted was eating the roof. This could only end one way. After a short while, Carrot Cottage began to list dangerously to the right as its walls gave way. Two seconds later, Ted came crashing down through the roof. He'd literally eaten the platform he was standing on. Very bright.

And the moral of this week's column? Don't punch giant bears in the face or eat your own house. Simple.

Chris Pascoe's Fun Tales

THE WRONG CAT TO FLIRT WITH

Ted's rabbit girlfriend Billie takes to courting the cat...

I'm in considerable pain at the moment, courtesy of a bad back that was probably partly caused by my being forced to spend 3,344 years on my feet at a London exhibition recently. I'm a very brave person with regards to pain – always ready to complain bitterly about every little knock and instantly assuming I'm having a heart attack every time I get mild indigestion, but on this occasion, my back really is bad!

Every time I attempt to straighten up as I get off the sofa I look like I'm going through the stages of a human evolutionary chart.

Ted, the World's Daftest Rabbit, seems to be at war with our giant feline Bodmin

Reaching human posture hasn't been possible for a few days now – I usually getting stuck somewhere around Cro-Magnon. This home imprisonment has forced me into spending a lot more time with a certain rabbit named Ted, the World's Daftest Rabbit.

This has been an interesting experience, not least because, on the odd occasion he's awake, he seems to be at war with the house's resident giant feline, Bodmin. Of course he is – why wouldn't Ted choose to declare hostilities on an iron-clawed killing-machine four times his own size and weight? It seems like a naturally stupid thing to do. Naturally Ted. The cause of this friction seems to be jealousy over Ted's live-in-partner-girl-rabbit →

Billie. Billie, always fond of Bodmin despite knowing Ted's never approved, has taken Bodmin's recent constant interest to mean he's taken a renewed shine to her (she thinks he wants to take her to dinner, whereas he actually just wants to make her his dinner).

Probably because of her mistake, and also because her best other offer is a mainly unconscious Ted, she's become incredibly flirtatious with the worst possible cat in the world to flirt with.

The situation progresses thus – Bodmin jumps onto the utility room worktop that the rabbit cage is situated on. Billie then sidles up to him through the bars, and Bodmin attempts to take her head off. Billie sees this as a romantic advance and presses still closer, something that's already resulted in her losing clumps of fur. When Ted wakes to witness all this courting, he becomes furious, jumping on and over Billie at pace and slamming headfirst into the bars.

This often has two immediate results – Ted bounces head over heels into his toilet tray, while a surprised Bodmin takes one step back and falls off the worktop. This sort of thing hasn't amused Bodmin at all and his attitude to Ted has changed dramatically lately – namely, he's totally furious and wants to kill him.

Because of all this, we've started lining the outside perimeter of the cage with Tupperware bowls full of water to stop Bodmin getting too close. I have to say that, despite my back pain, I've found myself marvelling at the sight of a large black cat attempting to jump from floor to worktop and pulling multiple bowls of water over his own head. He'll repeat this up to five times a day.

Which of the two did I say was stupid?

Chris Pascoe's Fun Tales

FANCY THAT!

Animal facts to make you go "wow"

The twisty, athletic leap rabbits make when they're happy is called a "binky".

Like cats, happy rabbits purr when they're content and relaxed.

Hedgehogs used to be known as urchins, which is how sea urchins got their name.

Cats have 24 more bones than humans.

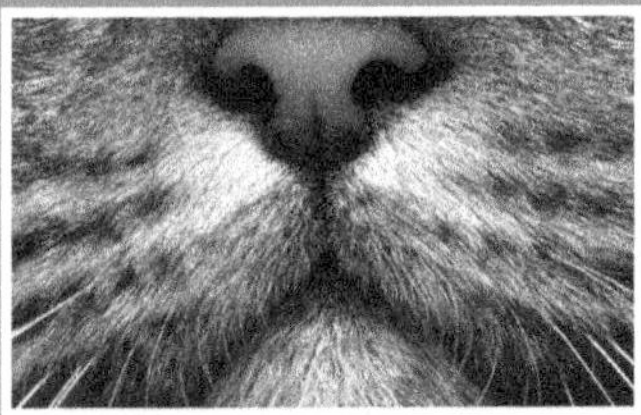

Cats have unique nose prints like fingerprints

Cows can walk up a flight of stairs, but once there they can't walk down again – their legs don't bend the right way.

Your dog's sense of smell is approximately 100,000 times better than yours.

A Day In The Life, by The Beatles, has a short section of audio that only dogs can hear

It's estimated that there are around 100 wallabies living wild in the UK in small colonies, including Devon, the Isle of Man, the Peak District and on an island in Loch Lomond.

A cat named Stubbs was elected Mayor of Talkeetna in Alaska in a write-in campaign in 1998. He reigned until his death in 2017, at the age of 20.

A group of rats is called a mischief.

Sheep have rectangular pupils which give them excellent peripheral vision – between 270 and 320 degrees.

PICTURES: ISTOCKPHOTO, SHUTTERSTOCK

Animal Crackers

Of course, torpid Ted isn't the only creature in Chris's life to cause him mirth and grief in equal measure. From catty cats to wally wallabies to rotund rats, there's a whole cast of furry friends and foes who ensure life is never, ever dull!

Chris Pascoe's Fun Tales

A STICKY SITUATION

It seems cats just can't resist turning Chris into something resembling Quasimodo!

My wife Lorraine is forever forcing me to "look after myself". Probably noting my failure to look after rabbits particularly effectively, she must feel the need to keep an eye on the situation. This enforced self-mindfulness can involve anything from putting a coat on in -10 degrees (she puts my reluctance to do so down to a Geordie gene in my heritage) to occasionally eating vegetables (really, I much prefer eating things that eat vegetables) and applying various creams and moisturisers before "it's too late". I'm concerned about what exactly happens when it's too late, but I resist the horrible oily stuff at all costs.

Every now and then though, Lorraine catches me totally unaware and slaps huge blobs of some cream or other onto my cheeks or hands. It was my hands she collared the other day, with the strict order, "just rub it in and stop complaining".

Stroking Jojo with moisturising hand cream, I found, was not a good idea

Well, that was easier said than done. No amount of hand rubbing would make it disappear. As I continued with my laborious task, my tortoiseshell cat Jojo jumped onto my lap and demanded to be stroked. Obviously, this was something I couldn't do while covered →

in sticky cream, but as her meows grew angry, I did so anyway, instantly regretting it.

One stroke and I looked like I was wearing a pair of wolf-man gloves, but one stroke was never going to be enough for Jojo, and realising she'd be getting no more, she turned haughtily on her heels and tail-flicked me in the eye. It was a spot-on strike. I grabbed at my running eye and was immediately stunned by the sting of two tons of hand cream plus fur.

Jojo, initially delighted to have caught me with a crafty hit, now jumped 3 feet in the air as I howled in pain, claw swiping me across the nose on the way down like a Kung Fu Panda ninja.

Now I was in a real mess, hunched over, bleeding from a gash across my nose, one eye wide open, the other half closed and streaming, like Quasimodo from the Hunchback of Notre Dame. Lorraine walked back into the room at that very moment and stopped in her tracks.

"The hand-cream," I rasped, holding my outstretched hairy hands towards Esmeralda – em, Lorraine – who recoiled in revulsion. She'd only left me two minutes ago, and all I had to do was rub in some moisturiser.

Believe it or not, this type of horrific transformation has happened to me before. On a catsitting pre-visit to meet a cat named Henry, the owner left the room to make a coffee while Henry and I got acquainted. Within seconds my ridiculously excitable new feline friend thrust his head into my face so hard I saw swirling stars. Moments later, he claw-kneaded my neck with joyous ferocity.

The stunned owner returned to find an unrecognisable man with scratches around his neck and a rapidly blackening eye...

Chris Pascoe's Fun Tales

MEAN MARSUPIALS

A wallaby in disguise is Chris's latest adversary from the animal kingdom

Given how often I write about a certain rabbit in My Weekly, you'd think by now I'd be able to recognise one, wouldn't you? But no, on a recent family outing to Whipsnade Zoo, and after watching a herd of some sort of weird African deer not gliding majestically over the Savannah, but standing stock still in a rain-soaked field, I happened to notice a rabbit standing a few feet behind them. As I studied the rabbit, I noticed something not quite right about it.

"That's a really big rabbit," I suddenly exclaimed, causing my daughter Maya to spill hot chocolate down her front. "It can't be a rabbit; surely, it must be a hare?" I continued. "No, no, it's definitely a rabbit – an absolutely huge rabbit!"

> "It's a wallaby!" Maya exclaimed. "How on earth could you think a wallaby was a rabbit?"

An extremely irritated and chocolate-coated Maya wrenched the binoculars from my hands, a move which, considering I had them strapped around my neck at the time, had me hurtling sideways towards her.

Maya studied the rabbit for a few seconds, the top of my head trapped at a 45-degree angle against her cheek, and finally gave →

out a huge exasperated sigh. "It's a wallaby! How on earth could you think a wallaby was a rabbit?"

Indeed. Humiliated by a wallaby then, and believe it or not, not for the first time. I have history with wallabies (that's a sentence you probably won't hear often). My Whipsnade wallaby woes go back 40 years, in fact.

On a forced school trip to the zoo in 1976, a free range wallaby stole my bag. As I sat on a hill, about to eat lunch, the bouncing marsupial appeared from nowhere, grabbed my bag and hopped off downhill at top speed.

Quarter of an hour, it took me to get it back, running back and forth across a muddy field in front of 30 jeering classmates. I did finally recover it, but only because the vindictive animal finally decided to drop it into a pile of muck so copious I'm guessing the elephants had been out for a morning stroll.

Add to all that, a wallaby I tripped over in Coombe Martin, Devon a few years ago and it's quite a picture, isn't it? What was a wallaby even doing in a Devon Dinosaur theme park anyway? I was looking up at Brachiosaurs and the like, not down… at wallabies.

Another thing about that particular theme park that baffles me to this day, is why they felt the need to have their animatronic dinosaurs double as slightly unsavoury impromptu water features. Still rubbing my knees after my wallaby incident, I stopped to admire a magnificent Tyrannosaurus, and it spat straight in my face. What an all-round lovely day that was.

And the moral of this story? Always remember rabbits are better than wallabies, and never trust a dinosaur from Devon.

Well, any advice from me was never going to be particularly useful, was it?

Chris Pascoe's Fun Tales

POND LIFE

Walking a paranoid cat on a harness can only lead to disaster...

"Oh, no," I stressed to my slightly annoyed catsitting client on the phone. "I'm certainly not saying Edcase is a nasty cat. I'm just saying he can be a bit feisty at times (read 'violently psychotic') and trying to take him for a walk might prove... problematic."

My client wouldn't be swayed, however. She often took Edcase for a walk on his harness, she told me, and he was fine about it. She also pointed out that he was never "feisty" with anyone else.

"OK," I conceded, wondering how Edcase came about his name if he really was all sweetness and light, "I'll definitely give it another try. It's just last time he gave me a bit of a nip (viciously imprinted his dental records on my forearm) but if you say he's fine now..."

As I desperately tried to help Edcase out of the water, he desperately tried to kill me

It all started well. Edcase allowed me to fasten his harness with nothing but an interested meow, before being happily led into the garden for his morning constitutional. So happy was he, he skipped ahead of me, and it was at this point my problems began.

As Edcase walked on, he suddenly became aware that somebody was following him. Me. He stopped dead in his tracks and looked suspiciously over his shoulder. I stopped too. Edcase took another couple of steps, and so did I – I had to. Edcase was now almost certain he was being followed. He tried another couple of steps and, his suspicions confirmed, swung round and hissed. →

Then, totally unexpectedly, he ran full pelt down the garden steps. Caught unawares and teetering dangerously on the top step, I had no choice but to go with him, running at breakneck speed down 15 steps before finally managing to bring myself to a halt just short of a fishpond.

The main problem with my sudden halt was that Edcase hadn't stopped, and instead attempted to vault over the pond and away from me. There could be only one outcome. His leash twanged tight and he dropped like a stone straight into the middle of the pond.

Now I was in big trouble. As I desperately tried to help Edcase out of the water, Edcase desperately tried to kill me. When he finally did manage to clamber onto dry land, his next move was to take a sudden bolt to the right, draping his lead around an ornamental cat statue, causing me to send it splashing into the pond.

As I watched the statue's face sink slowly out of sight, I couldn't help but feel things weren't going that well. Two cats in a pond in two minutes – that's a record even for me.

After a lot of pulling and begging, I finally managed to get an absolutely livid Edcase back into his kitchen. I won't go into too much detail about my efforts to remove the harness. Suffice to say that I did, and Edcase was soon happily purring again while I hunted for some plasters.

Cats hunt me, I hunt plasters. It's what we do.

Chris Pascoe's Fun Tales

HARD OF HEARING

Chris's additional communication difficulties continue... but relief is at hand

After last week failing to convince my local hospital to syringe my ears before they were ready to be syringed, I found myself facing another week of almost total deafness. After initial household anger at my lack of hearing – and I quote my teenage daughter Maya here, "IF YOU CAN'T HEAR, THEN DON'T SPEAK!" – both humans and pets became used to my situation and began taking advantage of it.

Maya would claim to have definitely received a "yes" to her chocolate bar request when I could have sworn she'd asked if I'd like a coffee.

> Jojo began jumping at me from all angles in much the way Cato attacked Clouseau

My wife Lorraine could chat on the phone about my shortcomings while I sat smiling benignly, wondering why Maya was taking so long with the coffee. Jojo the cat suddenly started jumping at me from all angles, in much the way Cato attacked Clouseau in the Pink Panther movies, delighted by my inability to hear her un-ninja-like approaches.

Meanwhile, Barry from a few doors down discovered my condition in the most ridiculous of circumstances. Emerging from →

Yeeeek!
Miaow

our cars at the same moment, we shouted our hellos. Then Barry shouted again.

"I can't hear you, I've gone deaf!" I bellowed, pointing at my ears. Barry seemed to understand as he responded by pointing at his own ears… but then he yelled again.

"No," I shouted, "I'm deaf!"

With that Barry shouted something else and began walking towards me. I walked towards him. As we reached one another, both still shouting, I realised Barry was trying to tell me that he'd gone deaf. It turned out he'd had the same ear infection, and was also smuggling olive oil within his auditory canal. We laughed in mutual understanding, each said something the other didn't hear, and went on our way.

Then, on Tuesday, the most wonderful thing happened. I went to the ear clinic, carefully on the lookout for enraged ambulance drivers and, after a brief inspection, was deemed all clear to have pints of water shot into both ears. As the water seeped away, I sat up unsteadily, and suddenly became aware of all sorts of weird sounds – the sounds of everyday life. I could hear!

"IS THAT OK?" said the nurse, her voice sounding like a cannon going off two feet from my right ear.

"Yes," I whispered, wondering how I'd never realised the world was such a loud place. I could even hear a clock ticking. It was fantastic!

Off I went on my cat-sitting rounds, in a state of near ecstasy. It proved a strange, very loud day. One cat mewed behind me and I almost jumped six feet over the sofa. Another hissed and I went looking for a gas leak.

Maybe the best part, though, was arriving home and hearing my daughter tell her friend that I'm a "good dad". She wouldn't have said that in a million years if she'd known I could hear her…

BEST FED RAT IN TOWN

A visit to his parents has left Chris shaking his head in wonder...

There are certain times in your life when you hear the words of a sentence but, so jarring are they, you struggle to fully take them in. The setting was my parents' home and we were all having a cup of tea. The perpetrator of the offending sentence was my mum and her exact quote was as follows: "Oh, I was meaning to tell you, I've accidentally been feeding a giant rat for the last two months."

You see? I was slightly dumbfounded to say the least. My dad meanwhile simply shook his head gravely and returned to his daily task of completely failing to finish his newspaper's cryptic crossword. I think the main problem is his point blank refusal to believe that cryptic clues really are cryptic. Anyway, how did Mum come to be providing regular meals for a giant rat?

"I thought he was a hedgehog," she explained. "He definitely used to be a hedgehog." My head spinning, as it usually is after a ten minute conversation with my parents, I asked how on earth this rat could have started life as a hedgehog.

"Don't be so silly Christopher," she admonished (I'm only called "Christopher" when I say something extremely stupid...)

"There was a hedgehog, and I was feeding him, but he's moved on and I thought it was strange how much more he's been eating lately, then the other day I looked out in the early hours, and there was a rat the size of a donkey eating his food." →

"A donkey?"

"A dog."

"Really? As big as a dog?"

"Well, a very small dog anyway; bigger than a Teacup Chihuahua."

"What's a Teacup Chihuahua?" I asked.

"It doesn't matter – what matters is that I've been feeding a giant rat for two months and I don't know how to stop."

I suggested that the simplest way to stop would be to not put food out, immediately causing my name to revert to Christopher.

"I thought I'd go and see Mrs Turnbull at number 15 about it."

Mrs Turnbull, the elderly ex-haberdasher ten doors down? What? Why would she go and see an ex-haberdasher about a rat?

> "Oh, I was meaning to tell you I've accidentally been feeding a giant rat for two months"

I felt my head begin to spin again.

"Why?" I squeaked, finding it hard to push the word out.

"Well, she's been having problems with rats for a long time. I thought it might be one of hers."

"Mum, you can't just return people's rats."

"That's what I've been trying to tell her all week, boy, but she won't listen."

With that Mum left the room with a "huff", presumably to put out some rat food.

Chris Pascoe's Fun Tales

IT'S BODMIN O'CLOCK

In the wee small hours, something very strange is afoot – Chris's brain!

Well, I'm writing to you this week from the Fronds of Nowhere. That's probably my strangest opening My Weekly line ever, but regular readers will have an idea what I'm talking about (which is more than my friends and family ever do).

I am of course referring to the fact I regularly send column ideas to myself via my mobile phone upon waking at around three in the morning, and consequently remind myself to write about things such as the Fronds of Nowhere, even though I have no idea what they are or what I was referring to when I wrote about them.

My underlying problem is that I wake in the early hours far too often, especially at this time of year with Christmas on the way and the clocks having gone back.

Apparently, I've got an "always-on brain", which is the exact opposite of what most people suspected. This means that after a few moments grogginess (presumably during which I message myself nonsense) I'm totally wide awake, thinking about the day ahead way too far ahead, and worrying about every silly little thing I can think of. This morning for instance I was fretting about the need to get a new artificial Christmas tree, having totally destroyed ours on its way back to the loft last year. Christmas is close but not so close I need to lie awake thinking of trees at 3am. But that's

MEOw!

the way I do things – my brain might be always on, but probably not for any useful purpose.

After sorting out my non-problems and finally drifting back to sleep, my – also always-on – massive ex-stray bruiser of a tomcat Bodmin will jump on my chest and meow full blast in my face, deeply concerned that I've gone back to sleep without feeding him. Such was the extent of this Bodmin problem we bought him a timer-feeder for his Christmas present last year. The Bodmin solution? He'd rip the thing open with his giant claws around midnight, eat the contents and then still jump on me in the early

My brain might always be on, but probably not for any useful purpose

hours. The timer-feeder was transferred to daytime usage and, thanks to its habit of sounding an alert for any interested felines seconds before opening, generally exploded its lid into our other cat Jojo's face as she rushed up to it. Cat-redundant, it's now in the possession of our rabbits Ted and Billie, and at least 50% useful (the Billie 50% of course).

I've just realised that within this week's column are two pretty good title ideas for paperback novels… The Fronds of Nowhere and The Bodmin Solution… and I'd definitely write those novels if I had any idea what to put in them.

Anyway I'm going to need to get back into a sleep routine in the next month or so – Christmas is an exceptionally busy time for catsitters. Those cats don't feed themselves, you know. Unless they're Bodmin at midnight, of course.

Chris Pascoe's Fun Tales

CHRIS TO THE RESCUE

Our intrepid catsitter is never afraid to go that extra mile to help his feline friends

I realised the other day that the vast majority of my friends are cats. Whilst this doesn't say much for my social skills, it does mean that when I see an old friend in the street, it's statistically likely to be one with pointy ears. This habit of bumping into cats in the street is a phenomenon that's become more and more frequent of late. I suppose, the more cats I have on my books, the more likely I am to meet one.

I was, for instance, driving through a local town the other day when I spotted a ginger cat standing on the pavement. I squinted for a second before suddenly pulling to a halt and proclaiming loudly to my wife Lorraine, "I thought so! That's Bob Jones over there. I haven't seen him for months." Lorraine stared at a pavement totally devoid of human life and, after a pause, finally reasoned that I wasn't hallucinating and must be referring to the small cat now staring wide-eyed at the car in that way cats have of making you feel your general appearance must be deeply shocking.

"Are you talking about the cat?"

"Yes, that's Bob Jones! Jackie Jones's cat, great to see him up and about; he hasn't been well!"

With that I was out of the door and heading for Bob, who with catlike predictability made me look a complete idiot by legging it through a hedge. I turned to look at Lorraine, who was now holding her head in her hands. →

BEEEEP! BEEEEP!
SPL
SCREECH

But Bob wasn't the first cat I'd seen in unfamiliar surroundings. I was visiting a lovely tortie named Mojo the other day, when I was a little surprised to see her sitting on the sofa cuddled up to a tabby named Benny. The main reason for my surprise being that Benny doesn't live with Mojo... or even in the same village, but rather a mile away and the other side of a wood. This was quite a revelation – the demure tortie and cavalier tabby, both of whom I've been visiting separately for over five years, unexpectedly know one other and are clearly friends.

Recognising cats can also have its heart-stopping moments.

I saw a Siamese cat appear from a clump of trees and sit down in the middle of the road

Driving locally one day, I saw a Siamese cat appear from a clump of trees and walk straight into the road and sit down.

I immediately recognised the cat to be one of my clients, Tom Arnold. With Tom sitting in the road and cars approaching at high speed, I knew I had to act quickly – against my better judgement I swung my car sideways across the road and put my hazards on.

Cars from both directions screeched to a halt with a great wailing of horns. As I picked up a bewildered Tom, I could just feel the love emanating from those cars.

The great thing is though, despite my valiant efforts I didn't actually manage to kill myself or any other road-user, and Mrs Arnold gave me a bourbon biscuit for my trouble. I usually only get Dreamies.

Chris Pascoe's Fun Tales

CAT IN THE DOGHOUSE

Being a prison guard for a mugger moggy is a dangerous occupation

Regular readers will know that, every now and then, violence erupts in our house and escalates into open warfare. Happily the violence isn't usually between humans (though my wife Lorraine can be a bit feisty).

I'll get to the point; Bodmin, our huge bruiser of an ex-stray tomcat, is currently grounded for attacking dogs.

He came in with a dog collar in his mouth a few days ago, prompting the dog's owner, from about 10 doors down, to leaflet the street saying, *Beware, a very big cat has been jumping on local dogs in their gardens.* There have been three incidents we're aware of.

Not good – and the fact Bodmin came home with a collar would suggest he's not only jumping on dogs, but robbing them too.

So until we can break his penchant for muggings (or muttings?), he's staying indoors. Chances are he'll eventually stop – he's declared war before, always eventually losing interest and moving on to different criminal activities.

His last grounding involved squirrels. Once Bodmin decides he has issues with something, it's like World War 3 out there. As squirrels all look so alike, I believe that even though there were about a dozen involved, Bodmin managed to convince himself he was constantly battling the one omnipresent squirrel. →

Naughty
Chair

Interestingly, he's never bothered a squirrel since, probably seeing them in his sleep by the time we enforced a peace treaty.

Obviously dogs are far from identical, so it must be that he's suddenly started resenting an entire species. Given that the collar we returned with heartfelt apologies was to a Labrador (a Labrador with a scratch on his nose), Bodmin doesn't seem to worry about the size of the dog either.

This latest grounding has its drawbacks; Bodmin has become very restless. He tends to become a bit "playful" when bored. For instance, just yesterday I beckoned our tortie cat Jojo to come and sit with me in the time-honoured fashion, tapping my hand repeatedly on my lap. I didn't see Bodmin on the wall unit behind me. To Bodmin, a bouncing hand is fair game, no different to a cat teaser stick, and so just as Jojo was about to jump, Bodmin dropped 3 feet through the air and beat her to it.

Eight kilos of muscular cat landed in a particularly sensitive place

Eight kilos of muscular cat landed in a particularly sensitive place, followed by a tortie who accidentally jumped on his back. Jojo shrieked in shock, but I have to say my own shout was higher pitched. Through watery eyes, I realised I'd now become a battlefield and my left hand was heavily involved, being held in a playful Bodmin death-grip while Jojo clawed his ears.

As quickly as it started, it was over, with both cats hurtling into the kitchen. Lorraine, alerted by the commotion, rushed into the room to find me curled in a ball, apparently in tears. With a shake of her head, she went back about her business – satisfied that my situation was the same as normal.

GIVING A HELPING PAW!

Does Chris need rescuing from himself... or from savage Spooky?

Most of the cats I look after on my catsitting rounds can be a little skittish at times – it seems to be a general cat thing. Cinders, for instance, is continually shocked to find she lives with a goldfish, Maggie finds teacups terrifying, while all four of Gazza's white paws leave the ground every time his owner's clock chimes, even though it's been doing the same thing, every hour, for eight years.

But quite often the most skittish and unpredictable of all are rescue cats. While some are so brilliantly balanced that you'd never know they've been through hard times in their lives, many can't help but show the scars.

At first Spooky played a clever game with us, demanding strokes and being irresistible

And I bear many of the scars too, especially after a week in which one lovely but very upset rescue cat, recently released from quarantine after an arduous journey from America, decided that I represented a "clear and present danger" and took to viciously attacking me at every opportunity. Note to self: shorts are NOT adequate clothing for a cat sitter.

One of my own cats, Spooky, is a rescue cat, something that

caused a little confusion when I explained the situation to my then-toddler daughter Maya.

Maya: Spooky's a rescue cat?

Me: Yes, that's right.

Maya: A RESCUE CAT! WOW! WOW!!

Me: Eh, why is that so amaz…

Maya: What does she have to do?!

Me: Do? She doesn't have to do anything. What do you mean?

Maya: How does she rescue people?! Who does she rescue?

An image of Spooky with a St Bernard's brandy barrel attached to her collar instantly sprang to mind. I liked the scenario a lot, but in the early days my relationship with Spooky was never as simple as a friendly stroke and a glass of brandy.

When we first visited her at the RSPCA she played a clever game with us, demanding strokes and being generally irresistible. Once home, it was quite a while before we saw any of that sort of thing again. She was a monster for weeks, particularly with me.

After a month of her gashing my hand every time a thought a quick stroke might be possible, I proved beyond any doubt how →

stupid I am (were there still any lingering doubts out there?) by putting my face to her instead of my hands.

Now while this might seem a little foolhardy, there was method in my madness. The terrified way in which she watched hands seemed to suggest she'd been hit by one in the past, so I hoped keeping my hands behind my back, and only approaching face-first might prevent her from panicking. My injuries were truly horrific. No, not really!

The gambit paid off – she brushed her face against mine and began instantly purring! But it was Maya who really rescued her rescue cat. Something in Maya's persistent attempts at friendship suddenly clicked with Spooky, and it's testament to the success of her full rehabilitation that, as I sit here writing this week's column, Spooky is lying on my desk and I'm typing around her paws!

Still no brandy though...

THE CANINE GUERRILLA

Chris relates a dismal encounter with a dog – and his links to an unfortunate footballer

I was bitten by a dog last week. This came as a bit of a surprise because, in my role as a catsitter, I hardly ever come into contact with dogs and while, cats being cats and I'm viciously scratched all day long, I'm very rarely bitten.

The dog in question was standing outside a local newsagents and, as I walked through the shop door, it suddenly launched sideways and bit me the back of my knee. This had a very painful and quite alarming effect – namely my suddenly appearing in the doorway of a crowded shop and shouting obscenities at the top of my voice while hopping from one foot to the other.

Nobody had seen the dog, so everybody assumed I was a lunatic. As I leant on the newsagent's counter, moaning, groaning and, ironically, panting like a dog, somebody finally asked me if I was okay. Pointing at the door I explained that a dog had bitten me on the way in, only for the shop owner to inform me that there wasn't a dog outside. I rushed to the door, just in time to see a tail disappearing round a distant corner. I still have no idea who that dog was, but he's certainly not on my Christmas card list.

When I got home, finally a little calmer and after putting up with my wife Lorraine laughing at my misfortune for five minutes (she's like that), the incident suddenly brought to mind an old story I'd heard about a 1960s goalkeeper named Chic Brodie. →

OUCH!
BUY-OUT

The reason this obscure story should come to me a result of a dog bite, was that Chic Brodie also had a very unfortunate "knee" incident involving a dog, but this was just the tip of the iceberg in the bizarre career of one of the unluckiest players ever to have graced the Football League.

In fact, Chic's knee was a target more than once – his bad luck story beginning with a member of the crowd throwing a stone at him, which hit him on the knee and ended with him being stretchered off the field. Not long afterwards, presumably not content with boring old stones, a spectator threw a hand-grenade at him. It turned out to be a replica, realistic enough for

As I walked through the shop door, the dog launched itself and bit the back of my knee

quick-thinking police officers to bury it in a bucket of sand. A few seasons later he jumped up and held onto the crossbar, something goalkeepers occasionally seem to do, but in his case bringing it crashing down onto his head and causing a half hour delay while he was stretchered off and the goalposts were fixed.

Then, just to cap it all off, the following year, a dog ran onto the pitch and Chic managed to run straight into it, tripping over and breaking his kneecap. As the great man himself said, "That dog might have been small, but it was solid."

Somehow I just know that, had I ever been anything more than an own-goal disaster at football, and had I ever managed to turn professional, my career would have mirrored Chic's in almost uncanny detail...

FIVE VETS & A MECHANIC

Chris ponders the problem of so many daft pets... and so many vet bills!

Our tortoiseshell cat Jojo had some teeth out last week and seemed fine, but she's been poking her tongue out at me repeatedly for the past two hours. She's either got it in for me today or something's gone wrong.

Something "going wrong" won't be a surprise in all truth. It's been one of those weeks when everything seems to go wrong at once. We've got two cars but neither of them work, the washing machine prefers to make strange gurgling sounds rather than wash clothes, and every pet in the house – bar Billie the rabbit and Bob the fish – has had a trip to the vets.

Firstly, Bodmin, our giant black ex-stray cat, decided to start pulling all his own fur out. While relieved that he had finally turned his attention on himself rather than the local dogs, off he went to the vets because there was obviously some underlying cause for this. There was; he's unhinged. OK, the vet didn't say that in quite so many words, but the inference was definitely there in the "calming pills" he was given.

Meanwhile, our death-defying strange little cat Spooky broke her leg – again – mainly through her refusal to accept that next door's roof can't be reached from our roof in one giant leap.

Ted, The World's Daftest Rabbit, lived up to his name by getting a blade of grass stuck up his nostril. So thoroughly did he manage to do this, they had to knock him out with anaesthetic to remove it. →

SMACK

Not wanting to miss out on the action, our other fish, Flash Gordon, suddenly decided he no longer wanted to swim in an upright position and started paddling along upside down. He didn't have to actually attend the vets, but we did need to ask them about him, and if you even say hello to a vet they'll charge you.

They diagnosed a swim bladder problem, prescribed some special fluid for the fish tank and suggested we pull him backwards through the water. He didn't like this at all, but it did seem to rectify the problem. Bob seemed to quite enjoy watching all this, probably pointing a fin and laughing at Gordon's rapidly receding furious face.

So anyway, with vet bills already climbing high, Jojo the haughty tortie began repeatedly punching herself in the face. At first we thought she must be taking a leaf out of Bodmin's book and picking fights with herself, but Jojo isn't really the fighting type. She once got slapped on the nose by a mouse and legged it.

Jojo isn't a fighter – she once got slapped on the nose by a mouse and legged it

So, having braved her tortie wrath by raising her chin and peering into her mouth, we realised she must be having problems with her teeth. After hugely expensive X-rays and tests, out came three teeth. Not content with that, we now have the aforementioned tongue poking thing going on, so it's back to the vets this afternoon.

I don't know why they don't just hold me upside down and shake me in case there's any loose change left in my pockets…

MEET THE PETS

An introduction to Chris's colourful cast of creatures

Bodmin 'Razorclaw' Pascoe

Bodmin simply moved in unannounced one day. The fact he just climbed in through the catflap, without ever being welcomed, is the only reason we feel confident he's not a vampire.

Age: Unknown. He didn't mention it on arrival.

Weight: 3.5 times that which could reasonably be expected.

Hobbies: Collar collecting, though the dogs he collects them from don't really appreciate it.

Main strength: Rodent "control".

Main flaw: The control of everything else that moves too.

Significant other: Billie the rabbit, though his intentions seem a little more murderous than Billie realises.

Enemy: Ted the rabbit. This is a love triangle.

Superpower: Leaping over 6 foot fences in a single bound, collar in mouth.

Ambition: Not to keep missing the fence-tops.

Summary: Dangerous psychopath. We like him a lot.

Jojo 'The Clown' Pascoe

Jojo is the princess of the group, and behaves accordingly (appallingly). She's almost constantly slightly angry, particularly with my daughter for naming her after a TV clown. Jojo demands total servitude from all.

Age: Princesses should not be asked their age (she's 12).

Weight: Princesses should most certainly never be asked their weight (2.8kg or one-third of a Bodmin).

Main strength: Using our bedroom as an obstacle course to somehow reach the top of the wardrobe at 3am.

Main flaw: Jumping on my head from the top of the wardrobe.

Significant other: Me! My wife Lorraine says Jojo seems to think I'm her husband.

Enemy: Spooky the cat, who refuses to acknowledge Jojo's existence.

Superpower: The ability to make every human serve her midnight snacks without understanding why they're doing it.

Ambition: To subjugate Bodmin and Spooky.

Summary: The greatest cause of sleep deprivation this side of the Arctic Circle.

Chris Pascoe's Fun Tales

Spooky 'The RSPCA Named Me' Pascoe

We broke Spooky out of prison in 2007, where she'd been serving time for getting lost without a microchip. When we visited her in the RSPCA D-Wing, she behaved so adorably we took her home. It was at least a year before she behaved adorably again.

Age: 13 plus however long she'd been without a microchip.

Weight: One-quarter Bodmin.

Main strength: A master fraudster, with the ability to completely hoodwink innocent visitors to the RSPCA.

Main flaw: Finally forgetting she was pulling a confidence trick and actually becoming adorable.

Significant other: All humanity. She seems to have become some kind of love-is-all-you-need hippy chick.

Enemy: All felinity. Her hippy culture doesn't extend to them.

Superpower: The ability to render Jojo completely invisible.

Ambition: World peace.

Summary: Seems very nice. We must assume that there was never trickery afoot and she definitely can't still be defrauding us after 13 years. Can she?

Chris Pascoe's Fun Tales

Ted's girl-rabbit is Billie, but he's always surprised to discover he lives with her

Ted, The World's Daftest Rabbit

A dozy rabbit who somehow, while mainly sitting completely still for 7 years, has had 3 books published about him – and counting!

Age: 7 years, but he's only been awake about 2.

Weight: Clinically obese.

Main strength: The ability to have no strengths whatsoever.

Main flaw: The ability to have no strengths whatsoever.

Significant other: Billie, his live-in-partner-girl-rabbit, but he's still constantly surprised to discover he lives with her.

Enemy: Running full pelt at Bodmin whenever he approaches hasn't really enamoured Ted to him.

Superpower: Falling sideways off shelves.

Ambition: To finally travel from the top of his hutch to the bottom without reaching terminal velocity.

Summary: Of no imminent threat – he may be staring at you for upwards of half an hour but still probably hasn't spotted you. →

Billie 'Cadbury's Bunny' Pascoe

This rabbit is the living embodiment of the term "long suffering". She lives in a hutch with Ted so no further explanation seems necessary, but when you take that thought a step further, you realise it also means she shares a toilet with him...

Age: 7 years, though she considers the day she moved in with Ted as "Year Zero". So 6.

Weight: Half a Ted.

Main strength: A back-kick so strong Thumper would be proud. Ted barely sees it coming.

Main flaw: Not finishing him off.

Significant other: While living with Ted, she's courting Bodmin; a very dangerous thing to do.

Enemy: Bodmin, if she ever gets close enough to nibble his gnarled ears.

Superpower: Lightning speed. If Ted attempts to get on her back, as rabbits do, she moves so swiftly he falls into thin air.

Ambition: A bigger hutch with a lockable toilet.

Summary: Extremely dangerous... if you're Ted.

Chris Pascoe's Fun Tales

'Lil Dog' Pascoe

Lorraine regularly sings along with my niece, to the tune of Tiny Tears, *Little Dog, Little Dog, Little Dog, Little Dog*, and now she's getting one. "What will you call it?" I asked. "Lil, of course... *Lil Dog, Lil Dog, Lil Dog...*" Oh dear.

Age: Unknown – we haven't broken her out of an RSPCA D-wing yet.

Weight: Hopefully at least one Bodmin, for her own protection.

Main strength: Weighing at least one Bodmin.

Main flaw: Not yet known.

Significant other: It'll definitely be Lorraine and my niece!

Enemy: I think we all know who that will be. She's going to need a good supply of collars.

Superpower: Lil is "Future Dog". Future Dog has the ability to appear in a book without yet existing.

Ambition: To be rescued by an adult and a toddler who'll sing about her all day.

Summary: Future Dog is coming soon!

Chris Pascoe's Fun Tales

'Bob-Along' Bob Pascoe

Bob is a fish who hates me. Despite my having been his main feeder for 10 years, Bob still turns his back on me whenever I approach his tank. He does this to nobody else, only me. Nobody knows why.

Age: 10, plus however long he was swimming around at Maidenhead Aquatics waiting for a forever home and somebody to hate.

Weight: Weighing him isn't an option.

Main strength: He has an excellent ability to express extreme emotion despite having no facial expressions.

Main flaw: Being a fish.

Significant other: Spooky the cat. If Spooky comes to the tank, Bob bobs.

Enemy: Obviously me. But I really don't know what I did.

Superpower: Self-necromancy, believe it or not. Bob appears to die about once a month, floating upside down, before bringing himself back to life. Interestingly he only "dies" when I'm approaching the tank.

Ambition: To cuddle Spooky without dying for real.

Summary: Bob is only a threat to himself.

Chris Pascoe's Fun Tales

Despite being his main feeder for a decade, Bob the fish seems to hate me

Christopher 'Calamity' Pascoe

I have no idea why, when I said I'd like to create profile cards for all our household animals, My Weekly automatically assumed that I'm an animal and so there'd be a me-card. But they did. And here it is...

Age: Look, do I have to do this? Yes? Oh okay, forty, cough, mumble, three.

Weight: As a reader once remarked my "dimensions of height and weight seem to have recently been reversed".

Main strength: The ability to lie about my age, underestimating by at least 10 years.

Main flaw: Giving my true age away a few lines later.

Significant other: Those on all the other cards.

Enemies: Those on all the other cards.

Superpower: I am ElectroMan! I build up so huge a static charge Bodmin thinks I have a secret weapon.

Ambition: Easy! Be super rich and good looking. The lotto can only help with the first.

Summary: I'm even more of a threat to myself than Bob.

...Pascoe's Fun Tales

Epic Failures

In truth, calamitous Chris really doesn't need any help from his motley crew of critters to make a fool of himself – he's quite good at doing that all by himself, thank you very much! Read on for yet more rib-tickling tales of mishap and misfortune...

Chris Pascoe's Fun Tales

WHAT A CLANGER!

Helping Maya with history revision has readjusted Chris's entire world view...

I have been revising for school exams over the last couple of weeks. Well, it's actually my daughter Maya's exams we've been studying for.

By "studying" I mean, I read out questions, she gives me the wrong answer, I correct her and she then shouts at me for believing the notes she'd written rather than the words she's now saying. It's as if she's having a full-scale argument with herself and I'm in the middle trying to break it up.

Something good about all this, though, is that I'm learning lots of new things. While with trigonometry I'd prefer just to keep on not knowing, my favourite topic has been history – in particular Alexander the Great, Cleopatra and dear old cuddly Hannibal.

Something I've really noticed is that many aspects of history aren't quite as I thought them to be. For instance, Alexander wasn't that great – he was a narcissist who killed his friends with spears during drinking sessions and went on to believe himself to be the son of the god Zeus.

OK, we've all dabbled in a bit of murderous self-deification in our time, but it's not really great, is it?

Hannibal probably wasn't that great either – he was just lucky enough to fight some really rubbish Romans. When he finally came up against a Roman who was quite good at fighting, he immediately →

Just a big a big a big
hunk o' love will do

got everyone around him killed – some of them because his own elephants charged at them.

And to cap it all the stunningly beautiful Cleopatra wasn't particularly beautiful. Her beauty just got embellished century after century until we ended up with Elizabeth Taylor.

All this prompted me to look up other anomalies in history – little things I'd always believed, but aren't true at all.

For instance, Christopher Colombus didn't discover the USA; only some Caribbean Islands. Joan of Arc, always held up as a hero of the French in their struggles against the English, was actually captured by a French army and sentenced to death by a French Bishop.

Maybe in revenge for getting the blame, one of Britain's first major attacks in World War Two wasn't on the Germans, but on the French Navy, sinking a large portion of it.

I've noticed that many aspects of history aren't quite as I thought them to be...

Staying with the French, Marie Antoinette never said "let them eat cake", and moving across the Atlantic, Benjamin Franklin probably didn't fly a kite in a thunderstorm – but simply suggested it would be a good idea.

Not one of the Salem witches was burned at the stake, Martin Luther probably didn't nail anything to a church door, and Nero didn't fiddle while Rome burned. There's no proof any of these things ever happened.

Also, JFK wasn't assassinated and now lives on the moon with Elvis and the Clangers. OK, that last fact may be from dubious sources, but the rest are apparently true. Amazing!

Of course, if Maya now fails history based on an essay about Elvis and the Clangers, I'm in seriously big trouble...

Chris Pascoe's Fun Tales

AY CARAMBA!

Chris's friend takes the phrase "lost in translation" to new and disturbing heights

I've recently had issues trying to speak in a foreign language. However, my friend Mia has been experiencing problems even worse than mine. Much worse.

Mia is a very clever young lady indeed, fluent in five languages. This not being enough for her, while on a backpacking trip through South America, she decided to learn Spanish. Her travelling companion Julie, an English girl (so obviously able to speak one language fluently – English) decided to have a go at Spanish too. While Mia's Spanish speaking abilities progressed at the speed of light – or rather, sound – Julie's did not, but that didn't stop her wanting to practice the new linguistic skills she didn't actually have at every available opportunity.

This habit caused a predictable amount of confusion, but none more so than when Mia and Julie attempted to book in to what appeared to be a budget hotel. Julie insisted that Mia took a seat while she approached the reception desk alone.

"I've got this one Mia," she said with a confident wink. Mia doubted that very much.

It's difficult to imagine exactly how the conversation went, but somewhere during the initial exchanges, Julie totally failed to realise that she was being told that this was not in fact a hotel at all, but rather, shall we say, a "house of ill repute".

She did however manage to convey that she'd very much like to take up residence, which was not a good thing to say at all. Mia, out of earshot, waved back at the proprietor as he grinned in her →

I've got this one Mia.
!
?

direction, a little over-enthusiastically she thought, but otherwise quite pleasantly. Perhaps things were going OK after all.

Or perhaps not. Mia watched as an argument suddenly broke out between Julie and the proprietor so she rushed over to join one of the most confusing conversations of her life.

"He quoted 30 dollars a night" whispered Julie, "So I told him no way, then he said OK, 35 dollars. I obviously said no, and then he put it up to 40 dollars!"

Mia was perplexed. How was Julie somehow managing to barter the price of a hotel room upwards? She decided it was time to take over, and so shook her head and, in her very best Spanish, said, "Forty dollars is too much."

"Too much?" he said, looking totally bewildered.

"Yes, much too much."

"How much do you think it should be?" asked the proprietor.

"He quoted $30 a night," whispered Julie. "I told him no way, so he then said $35!"

Mia looked around, summing up the tired decor and threadbare carpets.

"Ten dollars," she said firmly, folding her arms for effect, "And not a cent more."

The proprietor seemed absolutely delighted. It was when he then asked if she'd like the money in advance, she realised that there may just have been a bit of a misunderstanding here...

See, it's not just me. Mind you, at least they had the presence of mind to leave quickly. I'd probably have been climbing out a window sometime after midnight...

SPEED FREAK!

Chris has a fast-paced encounter with a member of the traffic police

I recently qualified for a Police Speed Awareness course. This isn't an achievement, as you only qualify for this by annoying the local police force.

While in most respects I'm a law-abider and usually stick to speed limits, I have problems getting up hills in my car, mainly on account of it being a bit rubbish. Therefore I have to pick up speed at the bottom of hills in order to arrive, quite a long time later, at the top. When there happens to be a speed trap at the bottom, I'm scuppered.

Strangely, I have a history of owning powerless vehicles. I once had a small motorbike that was so slow, a friend of mine walked past me with a cheery wave, while I was at full throttle. In fairness, that was on a very steep hill indeed. If we'd been on the flat, I'm pretty sure I could have pulled away.

My dad once saw me coming up our street on my motorbike and had time to nip indoors and come back out again just in time to wave an ironic chequered flag (tablecloth) in front of me, much to the mirth of our neighbours. Thanks, Dad.

Anyway, the speed awareness course, while at first feeling a bit like a short term prison sentence, proved to be really eye-opening, with the Police Trainer giving lots of hints and tips on situations such as being "bullied" into speeding by impatient tailgaters and on how to form speed-regulating habits.

Unfortunately he didn't give any tips on how to get up hills in rubbish cars. Overall though, it was a great talk and convinced me →

never to speed again. In return I convinced the trainer that I wasn't quite the full ticket. Or even the full speeding ticket.

I first came to his attention when he asked our group, in a conspiratorial way and with a wry smile, "Tell me this, when would most people slow down? When they're passing a school or when passing a police station?"

Ah, a clever question, I thought. He's making the point that people are more likely to obey the law – not when it's the right thing to do, but when there's a risk they'll get caught.

I called out, with a sage nod, "Police station!"

He looked sharply in my direction.

"What? That's ridiculous! Do you think policemen hang out of the window waving speed guns around?"

With that he shook his head in exasperation and the matter was closed. But I think I'd done enough to make him aware of me.

Dad waved an ironic chequered flag at me, much to the mirth of the neighbours

Being a nice chap though, he did shake my hand at the end of the course and we exchanged a few pleasantries. My closing goodbye sentence could, with hindsight, have been better... "Thanks again – I'd better zoom off, I'm late for picking up my daughter."

As I walked back to the car, I realised with a cringe exactly what I'd just said.

As I drove away, I noticed he was watching me like a hawk. He wasn't waving a speed gun, though.

CHEERS, WALT!

Chris pays a heartfelt tribute to his late father-in-law, a veteran at beating the odds

It's been about a year since my father-in-law Walt died, and since then his health has been greatly improved and he's been much happier and livelier. An odd statement, I know, even by the standards of this column, but regular readers may remember that Walt only actually died for five minutes. He then confounded medical science and stunned his doctors by spluttering back to life at odds of around a million to one.

At roughly the same time, his favourite football team, Leicester City, won the English Premiership. I'm not sure which scenario was the more unlikely, but I'd certainly like to have had a £1 accumulator on them.

Difficult bet to place down at the bookies, though... "Hello, I'd like to place a £1 bet on the Premiership title. Oh, actually can you make that a double and add my father-in-law coming back to life?"

Anyway, Walt was as right as rain after he died, and the doctors said that remarkably, he was actually in far better health than before it happened – a diagnosis Walt was never quite sure about, what with this annoying ailment and that, but he had to agree that the biggies, like angina and diabetes, had mysteriously vanished.

He then confounded medical opinion yet again, by promptly dying. Spike Milligan's epitaph "I told you I was ill" springs to mind. Walt was always one step ahead of the doctors.

Walt died peacefully in his sleep, and this time didn't bother coming back. I think he was ready. He'd cheated death so many times already, not least when he fired a 25lb mortar shell at himself →

Cheers!

(and at General Slim, of all people) while in the Royal Artillery, and almost drowned in the North Sea off the coast of Norfolk, only to be saved by what he perceived at the time to be a mermaid, but actually turned out to be a local girl out for a walk. And, of course, the above, when he cheated death for real.

This time, I think he decided he'd better not risk staying out any longer and should get back to his beloved wife Beryl, in a far better place to be.

The amazing thing is that he did so much good in his bonus year of life, it seems like he stayed around on purpose, purely to sort a few things out. Outstanding among those "things" was that, at the time of his first death, the family was in a bit of a fragmented state,

Walt rallied the family with a weekly outing to a local fish restaurant

with brothers and sisters having fallen out of regular contact.

By rallying everyone to him, first at his bedside and then via a weekly outing to a local fish restaurant, he pulled everyone back together, and his legacy is a now thoroughly re-bonded family. He knew what he'd done – on the last fish 'n' chip outing, he suddenly raised his mug of tea and said, "To a happy family." His mission was complete.

So, we salute you Bombardier Bakewell of the Royal Artillery. And thank you for everything.

Chris Pascoe's Fun Tales

TERMINAL VELOCITY

Chris's wife is seriously unimpressed with his drone piloting skills

Every now and then, I do something really stupid. OK, regular readers, I know you now have one eyebrow raised. How about, around once a month I do something really stupid? Still understating it? Fair enough, I suppose. My daily routine is: get up, have breakfast, do something completely stupid, have tea, go to bed. Satisfied? You're right, of course.

Even by my standards though, what I've been up to this week is another level of stupid. I purchased a drone. In fact I bought two drones. Seduced by the whole idea of being able to effortlessly fly a small aircraft without killing myself, I went to my local geek shop and bought a tiny little four-pronged helicopter.

Before flying it, so alien to me was this thing, I performed the very un-me-like action of reading the instruction book. Unfortunately, these instructions didn't tell me that the drone had a barely distinguishable front and back. Not only that, but your remote control handset would work in complete reverse if it took off the wrong way round.

Mine, of course, took off the wrong way round. My drone lifted six feet off the ground, hovered for a few seconds and then, as I gently pushed my joystick forward, flew straight into my face at high speed.

I crumpled to the floor as if someone had taken the stopper →

VROOM!

out of one of those inflatable wobbly-armed giants you see flailing around at various sales events.

As I went down, the drone went up… and up… and up… mainly because I was unwittingly pressing the joystick that way. Scrambling to my feet, and in a moment of sheer panic at the incredible height my drone had reached, I switched off the remote control.

Once off, the remote is unable to take back control even if switched back on. Things were not looking good.

The drone stopped for a second, up there near the stratosphere, realised it was now on its own and its idiot pilot had bailed out and, in the terminology of the late great Douglas Adams, glided gracefully to the ground "in much the same way a rock doesn't". Also in Douglas-speak, "the art of flying is to throw yourself to the ground – and miss".

The drone hovered for a few seconds and then flew straight into my face at high speed

The drone didn't miss. It hit the ground at such terminal velocity that I'm still finding bits of it days later.

So, what do you do when you've proved yourself to be totally incapable of flying even the tiniest of drones? That's right, you go out and buy one around twenty times its size. My reasoning was that, being bigger and apparently better, it'd be much easier to control.

In my mind, I can still see my wife Lorraine's face as she stood at our bedroom window and watched in amazement as a football sized drone flew straight at her at top speed and disintegrated as it thumped into the double glazing right in front of her nose.

She was impressed, I could tell. So impressed in fact, that our garden has now been declared a no-fly zone for the foreseeable future…

Chris Pascoe's Fun Tales

WHAT A HOWLER!

Chris recalls his call centre career... and the co-worker who gave customers an earful!

I've written before about my short but "lovely" stay in a market research call centre. Even glancing at that sentence brings back so many memories, but after a stiff drink I've managed to get over those, and remembered some goods one too.

I'll start with the worst though. A girl I worked with liked to moan. She moaned about the chairs, the desks, the temperature, but most of all, the headsets we wore when making calls.

"Filthy things," she complained to me one day, "You could catch a nasty infection off these filthy things. Blooming filthy."

"No, no," I reassured her, "They're fine; I've been using them for ages with no problems at all."

Two days later I caught a really vicious ear infection and had to go to hospital. In the hospital waiting room, I couldn't help but notice something totally wrong with the queuing system.

It's an ear clinic, yes? Every patient in the waiting room is suffering with something ear related. We must assume that the majority, like myself, are having some problem with their hearing. So the nurse appeared at regular intervals, stood behind everybody and, in the quietest voice possible, called out something along the lines of "Mr Smith to Room 5 please." Nobody moved. "Mr Smith?" she'd whisper again. Nothing. Magazine pages turned, nobody stood up.

→

RRRAAAAAAHHHHHH-
OOOOOOOOOH
OOOH!
OOH!!!

I truly believe some of those people must still be sitting there today.

I just about heard my own name and eventually received the bad news that it'd take a month to get my hearing back. The good news was, you can't talk on the phone if you can't hear anything. It was a month off for me!

Moving on to the good memories, a great one was my colleague Mia. When Mia first arrived from Italy, she had a few problems getting acquainted with everyday English. Consequently, when our boss John gave us all a stern reprimand over our poor performance levels, Mia thought she'd break the silence and up John's mood by complimenting him on his colourful trouser braces.

"I really like your suspenders John," she said shyly. Easy mistake to make, I suppose. The room erupted in laughter. John had Mia's card marked from that day forward.

"I really like your suspenders John," Mia said shyly as the room erupted in laughter

A few weeks later, during a musical survey, Mia puzzled over how to categorise "traditional Brazilian dance music" and put her interviewee on hold.

"Brazilian anyone?" she suddenly shouted to a near silent room.

John's head raised from his desk. "Brazilian? Please?" she stood up and bellowed. A silent John added further notes to Mia's file.

After a few more incidents, including one where she completely misunderstood a client's question and attempted to demonstrate into her phone exactly what a howler monkey's call sounds like, Mia finally got fired.

In case you're wondering by the way, a howler monkey's call is loud. Very loud indeed.

Chris Pascoe's Fun Tales

HEROIC FAILURE

Chris delves into history and finds a typically slapstick tale of maritime misery

On a recent trip to the new Mary Rose museum in Portsmouth's Historic Dockyards (housing one of the most breathtakingly awe-inspiring exhibits I've ever seen, by the way) I discovered a historical misconception that's been confusing me for 30 years.

The sinking of Henry VIII's flagship, the Mary Rose, has always been a strange one for me. Every time I hear her story, it's changed dramatically.

Initially, at the time of the Mary Rose's 1980s salvage from the stretch of sea between Portsmouth and the Isle of Wight, I'm sure I saw news reports saying very clearly that it "was lost on its maiden voyage in 1545, capsizing and sinking in full view of Henry Vlll, who was watching from the shore." I also remember thinking what an incredibly rubbish way that was to go down. In the dockyard where she finally came to rest, you have the gallant HMS Victory, battered and bruised hero of Trafalgar, and the incredible HMS Warrior, a Victorian warship so fast, tough and thoroughly tooled-up that enemy ships surrendered without a shot being fired, and then the Mary Rose – who fell over.

Then, a few years ago, during the Mary Rose's long renovation period, I read that she wasn't on her maiden voyage when she sank at all, but had in fact already served in the Navy with distinction →

for decades. So that was an altogether differen'
the same ending though – simply toppling over in
Henry.

Then, on the aforementioned visit to the museum the
day, I finally heard the true story, and it left me stunned. She did go down in battle after all, and not just in any old battle, but rather facing off a huge French invasion fleet that was twice the size of the Spanish Armada.

"The Battle of the Solent" was a huge confrontation that I'd never heard of, and apparently, neither have most people. During the battle, the French even invaded the Isle of Wight. What! The French invaded the Isle of Wight? How dare they!

Amazingly, the whole thing has since been largely forgotten by history – though probably not by the Isle of Wight residents who had their houses burnt down that day. You tend to remember that sort of thing.

I remember thinking what an incredibly rubbish way that was to go down

While all this was going on, the Mary Rose was closing in, bravely leading her fleet into battle. Okay, she did still fall over and sink, but not without good reason.

The Mary Rose rounded on the French fleet and fired an impressive cannon-broadside, before beginning a turning manoeuvre to fire again. Unfortunately, a huge gust of wind caught her full on, causing her open cannon ports to dip beneath the waves and take water in at an alarming rate.

There was nothing anyone could do, except sink of course, which they did without delay.

So, Mary Rose, I'm so sorry for my earlier opinion of you. You went down bravely and you went down fighting. HMS's Victory and Warrior should be very proud.

Chris Pascoe's Fun Tales

RADIO HA HA!

Barmy broadcasting from a local radio station is music to Chris's ears

I recently went off for a weekend away with my wife Lorraine and daughter Maya, and came across a local radio station that made our own local station seem like the very benchmark of broadcasting. Sitting in our hotel room and staring out to sea with a beer (one of the few things I'm good at) I switched on the radio and within five minutes found myself staring at it aghast.

Firstly, the presenter mentioned in passing the sinking of the Titanic, only for his co-host to enthusiastically interject that he'd read "over twelve people drowned that day". Really? Twelve? How did the other 1,491 meet their doom then?

The presenter wasn't going to accept that as fact though, stating that he was sure the numbers would have been in the high thousands and instructed his production team to check the figure. "No" came the immediate response.

That "no" would appear to have been final, because we didn't hear anything more about it.

A few minutes later, during *Love Me Do* by The Beatles, the presenter could clearly be heard talking in the background. "You're a moron" he shouted in his strong West Country accent, "A total moron, from a whole line of morons… a lineage of morons… a moron lineage."

I shook off the notion that the attack might have been personal, reasoning that he couldn't possibly know I was listening. The Beatles carried on playing with no further interruptions, but as soon as the record finished, the presenter continued his perfect five →

You're a moron!
100.0
2 Band Receiver

minutes of broadcasting with the unexpected line: "Well, that was Blur there with their big hit *There's No Other Way.*"

No it wasn't.

"And next up, here's Rick Astley with *Never Gonna Give You Up*.

There followed 30 seconds of deafening noise which had me grabbing for my ears and Maya frowning over the top of her phone. When the thunderous burst of static subsided, I distinctly heard somebody shout the word "moron" before we were treated to a second playing of *Love Me Do*... immediately followed by a full minute's silence.

It had been the most breathtakingly wonderful ten minutes

When the thunderous burst of static subsided, I heard someone shout, "Moron!"

of radio I'd ever heard. Disappointingly, the next hour proved blooper-free, and actually quite good, but they weren't quite finished yet – the presenter wound up his show, his co-host cheerily shouted goodbye to their "lovely wholesome audience", and right on cue, they went straight to the adverts, but not before the words, "My God, that was flipping awful!" could be heard drowning out the station's signature ditty.

Very true, I suppose, but also, totally flipping brilliant!

Chris Pascoe's Fun Tales

I A-DOOR YOU!

You will be able to see right through Chris's latest madcap adventure...

It's good to have doors. While that opening sentence is about as blindingly obvious as it's possible to be, I don't think I ever realised just how great doors are – until I didn't have any, that is. So, why did my house suddenly become so startling open-plan that it didn't even have any doors? It all started when my wife Lorraine chose a new set of internal doors to replace the filthy lumps of rotting wood we've had hanging off every door-frame for the last two decades.

A carpenter, who I have to say was absolutely excellent (I have to say that because he told me to... and also because he is excellent) then came along, took all our old doors off and got called away on an emergency (not sure what emergency carpentry involves), leaving us with no doors for 48 hours.

While that sounds like a very minor thing, it's very hard to describe the strangeness of being in a house without doors.

I first realised that subtle lifestyle changes had taken place when I was clandestinely raiding the kitchen chocolate cupboard and Lorraine called out "remember your diet" from the bathroom.

She could see me from the bathroom. In fact, we could all see each other from everywhere. Bodmin, our giant bruiser of an ex-stray tomcat intently watched my every move around the house with a look of narrow-eyed hatred (he didn't mean anything by it, →

Ted the rabbit could suddenly see down the length of the house

it's just the only facial expression he has) while Ted the rabbit could now see down the whole length of the house from the garden.

It's testament to Ted's total lack of interest in anything but hay that he turned his back on his newfound view of the world and stared at the back of his hutch wall for two days.

I realise I'm not very interesting to look at, but apparently a single piece of blank plywood has more crowd appeal. Great.

Noise was another problem. With my daughter studying for school tests, I was shushed whenever I spoke, even from the other end of the house. In fact even my walking silently past her door-less bedroom became a major annoyance.

Also, my normal crashing and clattering around the house distracted Lorraine from her reality TV shows, unable to shut the lounge door because there wasn't one. Reality interrupting reality.

So, with a house offering the opportunity to see me from every angle, I discovered that nobody wanted to see me unless I stole chocolate (except a glaring cat of course) and nobody wanted to hear me speak unless... um, well, just nobody wanted to hear me speak.

After a history of disastrous book-plugging interviews, many radio stations were already well aware of that fact, even if I wasn't.

Luckily, the new doors are in place now, and we can go back to happily ignoring each other like all good families should.

Life's always best when you can eat chocolate without heckling from the toilet...

FANCY THAT!

Disaster facts to make you go "wow"

In 1962 Decca Records believed that guitar bands would be a 5-minute wonder and declined to sign new group The Beatles.

Western Union turned down the opportunity to buy the patent for the telephone – they couldn't see how they could make money from it.

The Washington Post polled a group of financial leaders and their predictions were published under the headline "Good Times Are Predicted For 1929" just before the Wall Street Crash.

There were only two cars in the whole of Ohio in 1895, and they crashed into each other.

In Liechtenstein's last military engagement in 1886, none of its 80 soldiers were injured, and 81 returned, with the addition of an Italian who had joined them.

Burt Reynolds turned down the part of James Bond in 1967. Hugh Jackman did the same nearly 40 years later and the role went to Daniel Craig.

Roman Emperor Calilgula once waged war against Poseidon. He led 10,000 soldiers to the sea and ordered them to stab it with spears.

Apple co-founder Ronald Wayne sold his 10% share of the company for £800.

In 1932, the Australian military were called in to cull emus destroying crops in Western Australia. After six days and 2,500 rounds of ammo, only a handful had been killed and the troops retreated.

Kodak was the first company to develop the technology for digital cameras and cell phones but decided to sit on it as it could threaten their existing business.

General J Sedgwick's last words, during the American Civil War were, "They couldn't hit an elephant at this distance" moments before being shot and killed

PICTURES: ALAMY, ISTOCKPHOTO, SHUTTERSTOCK

WAKING UP IN POUNDLAND

From a sinus wash to a discount supermarket – it could only happen to Chris

I am, as I'm sure quite a few readers are, part of the "Sandwich Generation," a term describing those of us who, while trying to get by in the world ourselves, find themselves caught between teenagers on one hand, and elderly parents who are pretty much on the reverse journey through teenagehood and back to childhood on the other.

My father has, in the course of one week, accidentally covered his kitchen in marker pen and opened his car door straight into a kindred spirit on a mobility scooter – typical toddler activities.

Meanwhile my teenage daughter Maya isn't exactly having problems of her own, more just a problem with me.

While I have to admit that most of Maya's complaints are valid, I do think I'm sometimes a little hard done by. For instance, in a supermarket recently, I caught the eye of a baby who obviously found my face hilarious so I went into entertainment mode and started playing peek-a-boo. Maya was horrified.

"Daddy! Babies don't have 'object permanence' so when you play peek-a-boo they genuinely believe that you've temporarily ceased to exist. It's really upsetting for them." Hmm.

And, while coping with parents and teenagers, I've had to deal with a few problems of my own recently. Some may remember that over the course of my columns here, I've had a throat operation →

and an ear infection. Well, just to complete my ENT triumvirate, I recently had to go into hospital for a sinus wash. I can honestly remember nothing from the moment I went under anesthetic, to coming round... not on a hospital trolley, but in Poundland.

Suddenly blinking to full wakefulness, I heard the words "Hello, hello, can I help you?" and found myself staring at a Poundland checkout operator with a dazed expression on my face, a huge queue forming behind me.

To complete the picture I was wearing a hospital identity bracelet and a tiny line of blood trickled from my left nostril. I must have looked like I'd escaped from somewhere very secure.

It's to the credit of the store supervisor then, that she gently led me away, her arm around my shoulder, and even gave me a little squeeze. See, now you think of sinus washes as quite romantic, don't you?

Suddenly blinking to full wakefulness, I heard the words, "Can I help you?"

When I finally got home, I found an answerphone full of messages from the hospital asking where I was. Apparently, despite my having no recollection, I'd been sitting up in bed following my operation, before getting dressed without permission and promptly vanishing. Why, in a zombie-like state, I would automatically head for Poundland, I have no idea.

Actually, forget the very young and the very old, some of us in the middle are a bit of a problem, too...

Chris Pascoe's Fun Tales

MY LIFE AS A HEAD-BANGER

Just as well that Chris wasn't destined to be a 19th century sailor

Last weekend, we finally took my parents to see the Mary Rose. After nearly 500 years, we thought it was probably about time.

I'd been looking forward to seeing their faces on seeing that 1500s battleship restored in such breathtaking fashion, and they were predictably impressed… well, Mum was. Dad seemed more taken with a skull in a glass case. Strange chap, my dad.

After the Mary Rose and a cup of tea, my parents decided to use their all-attractions ticket to wander around HMS Victory, just across the road.

Now, whereas the Mary Rose is in a big, spacious, modern, safe environment (though not very safe for whoever's skull was in that case), HMS Victory is most certainly not. In 2018, the Victory is almost exactly the way it was in 1805 – full of steep rope-ladder steps, slippery decks and very low beams in unexpected places.

On my own visit last year, I managed to smack my head six times in the space of 20 minutes, much to the enjoyment of my teenage daughter who unbeknownst to me, after the first two strikes, started videoing me, knowing she was producing comedy gold for her friends.

How marvellous that she considered a tour around such an incredible piece of British history not nearly as important as filming →

OOUUCCHH!

a man repeatedly banging his head on the ceiling. Anyway, my point is that, if I managed to do all that self-damage, there was no saying what my dad could achieve. But, being tight-fisted, I didn't have an all-attractions ticket and so wasn't able to accompany them. All I could do was wave them off with a recommendation not to die.

Almost two hours later, I sat nursing a fifth cup of tea staring at HMS Victory and wondering if my parents were ever planning to come out. My wife and daughter had long since abandoned me for a shopping trip, so I decided to annoy my friend Mia (she of previous column notoriety) by texting my concerns to her. Under a photo of the Victory, I texted, *Waiting for my parents to come out, or just as likely, an ambulance to go in.*

My teenage daughter began to video me, knowing she would capture comedy gold

Mia, clearly waiting expectantly for messages from me, replied three days later with the line, *Well! I'd had a gin or two, but when I first looked at that ship I thought you were collecting your parents off some cruise!*

Some cruise, indeed. To Trafalgar and back, half the crew dead, and 212 years back in port. Actually, that sounds exactly like the sort of cruise my parents would have ended up on.

Just to be clear, I wasn't still waiting at the Victory when Mia's reply arrived, though it felt like it. When they finally came out, Dad was in considerably better shape than I'd been. I'd clearly underestimated him.

"That was amazing!" he said. "Going by the mess it looked on the outside, you wouldn't believe the Mary Rose looks like that inside!"

No. No, you wouldn't...

Chris Pascoe's Fun Tales

DOWNLOAD OVERLOAD

Brains, computers… what's the difference with them in the end?

I was thinking the other day, with my brain coincidentally, about how much the human brain resembles a computer. Let's start from the beginning. Our brain has very basic functions up until the moment of birth (our start-up routine) that enables it to be switched on and immediately start downloading software.

And wow, do baby's brains download – they can even learn multiple languages at the same time (in my case those languages happened to be a strange form of lazy English mixed with a smattering of Gibberish, but it's possible apparently!).

All very computer-like then, and this trait continues into childhood, with toddlers' brains possessing far quicker learning capacities than their adult counterparts, which in computer terms, are by then far too clogged up with cookies. Each day, as bugs and glitches start to occur (brain getting tired), it becomes necessary to, in the best traditions of computer maintenance, "switch it off and on again"... so we go to sleep.

A few hours later, back on it comes, fully re-booted and in my case, eager to download some more of those cookies. Eventually, as the brain progresses through its teens and into its twenties, it may start downloading "viruses" that cause brief malfunctions. Just like their computer counterparts – trojans, worms etc – these viruses have famous names, such as Stella, Tennent's and Bell's. ➙

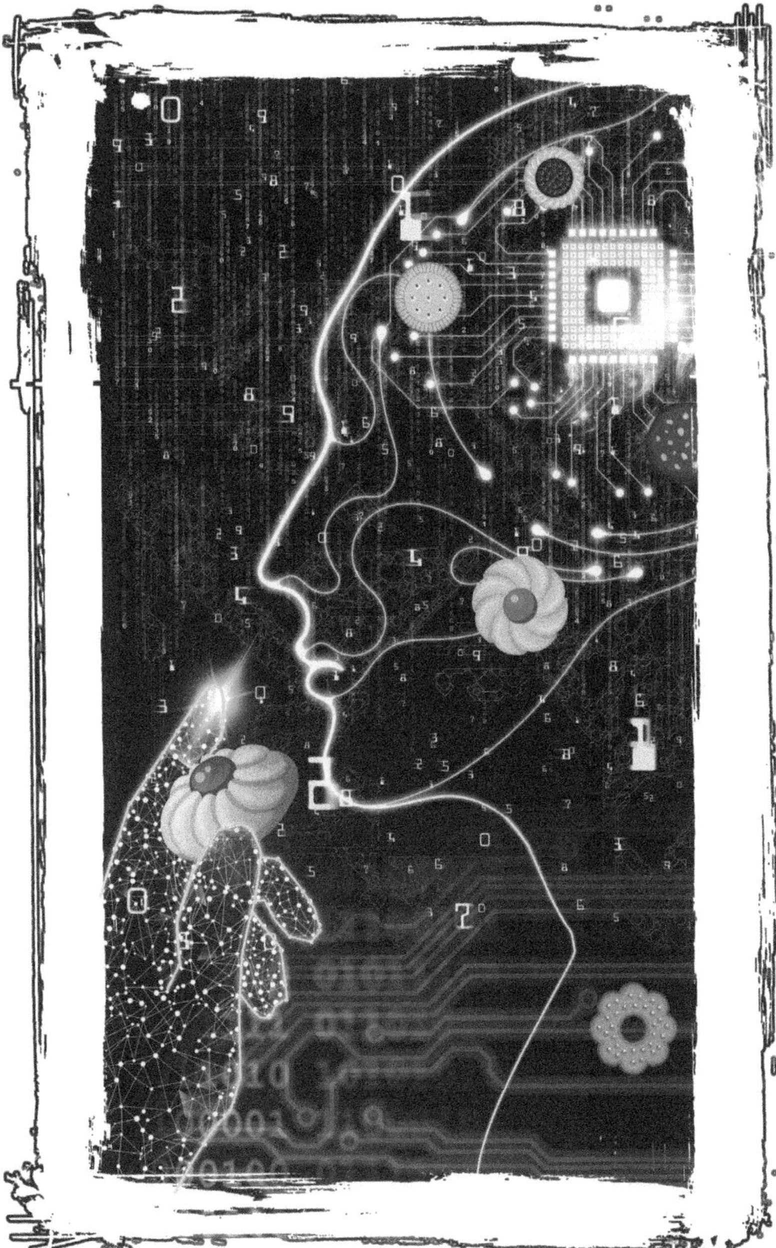

Sometimes these viruses necessitate a full system clean out, usually performed face-first over a toilet, but generally a good night's re-boot does the trick.

When computers get old, of course, they can start developing a few problems in the memory department, and often get themselves into some fairly strange sub-routines which make absolutely no sense to anybody but themselves. No similarity to humans there then… When these memory issues occur, it becomes a good idea to download all vital information to a mini version of itself, or a data-stick. Stand by Maya Data Stick.

But we should never forget (or at least our Memory-Mayas should never forget) that it was the human brain that invented, or gave birth, to computers in the first place... so not only is the brain like a computer, it's the mother of all computers.

So in that sense, the brain must be superior, mustn't it? But then,

> Adult brains, in computer terms, are by then far too clogged up with cookies

think about it; exactly what just told me that brains are superior? Hmm.

Just to finish off here, and sticking with the IT theme…while booking a break to the Isle of Wight recently, I was told that the Isle of Wight is the largest of Britain's many islands. Quite interested by this, I asked our old AI friend Alexa exactly how many islands Britain has. Her answer stunned me – apparently there are over 6,000 (where are they all?!). I then asked how many of these were actually inhabited. Alexa obviously misunderstood my question slightly, because she replied, and I quote, "There are over 17,000 human settlements in the British Isles."

What worries me is.. what settlements other than "human" settlements do we have here? Gulp…

Chris Pascoe's Fun Tales

OUT WITH A BANG!

Chris hears some new hair-raising wartime stories from his father...

Because my dad is now getting on a bit, and recalls World War One far better than he recalls last Thursday, we tend to have quite a few chats about his life in Portsmouth during the 1940s.

Given my family's historical lack of luck, it's really no surprise that my father should have spent his war years in Britain's premier destination for Luftwaffe pilots, spending many nights in his family's above-ground Anderson air-raid shelter, offering virtually no protection against falling bombs. And when that was all over he moved to Slough, a town that the Poet Laureate John Betjeman suggested should be razed to the ground: *Come friendly bombs, and drop on Slough; It isn't fit for humans now.*

Things really weren't great, were they? Chatting about all this, as we do many mornings while I'm trying to work out how my mum's managed to accidentally deactivate Sky TV and disconnect the internet, I mentioned Dad's own father, as once recorded here, being blown 30 feet into the air complete with his pushbike and air-cycling straight into a wall.

Totally unexpectedly, Dad replied, "That annoyed him, that did. Not as much as his shed did, though." The reason this sentence came as such a surprise was that, although we've talked about most things upwards of a thousand times, there had never before been →

BOOM!

any mention of a shed. Especially one that was more annoying than cycling into a wall.

"His shed?" I asked. "What was wrong with his shed?"

"Nothing was wrong with it… well, not until it got blown up, anyway." So, this was new – Grandad's shed was bombed!

"He'd only just finished building it the day before, and we were standing out in the road watching the bombers, when suddenly, our shed blew to smithereens. There were bits of shed raining down on us, and we were right down the street. Mr Henderson got hit by our watering can."

All this sounded about par for the course, but one question immediately sprang to mind. "Why were you standing in the road in the middle of a bombing raid?"

"Oh, we used to like watching the dogfights [so not in the Anderson shelter after all then?]. I saw a Messerschmitt pilot

Mr Henderson got hit by our watering can as bits of shed rained down

parachute into the sea one night. Great big cheer went up when that happened, I can tell you!"

A big cheer? So they were all out there in the street then. Health and safety back then probably wasn't what it is nowadays. As if to emphasise this, Dad continued, "That was the night they got Woolworths. All that was left was the lift shaft. Many a happy day us kids spent, climbing up to the top of that shaft."

Somehow, that didn't surprise me, but one thing certainly did… the fact Woolworths existed in World War Two. Really? I looked it up. We had Woolworths in World War One, never mind Two.

You see, this is why I should never have been allowed to write a history book.

Chris Pascoe's Fun Tales

CATS, DOORS & MISSING GNOMES

Chris has no trouble looking after cats – it's the humans who cause problems...

Every now and then, through my ability to make any given problem much worse, I get myself into situations that border on ridiculous. In fact, they go over that border by quite some way and wander around in the fields of absurdity.

I mention this only because I've been there this morning. Upon arriving for a first visit at a catsitting customer named Mary's house, and having made small-talk with the resident feline while preparing his meal (actually, me small-talking, him shouting at me), there was a knock at the door.

The strange thing was, it was at the back door, which led only to an inaccessible garden. At least, I thought it was inaccessible... but the old chap from next door had walked straight through the hedge. "Morning!" he boomed, "I'm Alf from number three. I was looking out my bedroom window this morning and I noticed Mary's patio door isn't shut properly."

With that, he put his hand on my shoulder and led me, or rather frog-marched me, to the offending door. It was indeed slightly open, and I attempted to slide it shut. "No, no, no," he shouted (why did everyone in this house shout, cat included?), "I tried that from the outside, it won't budge."

After a lot of experimenting it became clear it was impossible to either slide the door shut or open it any wider than six inches. We decided to phone Mary. It was here that things went badly wrong... →

Morning!

Me: Hi, Mary, I'm having a problem shutting your patio door, it won't...

Mary: I know about that – is it in the locked position though? It's fine if there's a gap because...

Alf (booming from behind me): A fat lot of good that is!

Mary: Sorry, Chris? Can you just let me finish my sentence...

Alf: If you can't shut it, it's not a door!

Mary: Look, could you please just let me speak?!

Alf (laughing): Bloody rubbish door!

Mary: Chris! Just listen!

I appeared to be taking part in an ever more heated argument with my customer, even though I hadn't actually said anything.

Me (to Alf but unfortunately straight into the phone): Can you just be quiet, please!

Mary: I BEG YOUR PARDON?!

I appeared to be in the middle of an argument without actually saying anything

You see... I'd managed to make things even worse. My redemption came in the form of a shouting elderly man.

Alf: Don't you tell ME to be quiet, young man!

Mary: Is there somebody there with you, Chris? Is that Alf from next door?

Phew. Thrown into trouble and rescued by the same man. Alf wasn't finished though. "Are you the lad who looked after Mary's cats last year?" he asked, squinting suspiciously at me. "The one who ran off with my gnome?"

"Yes, I am," I replied, before fully registering his second question. "What? No, I mean, yes, but I didn't take a gnome!"

"Hmm," he muttered, and with that, he was gone. Chris Pascoe, abusive catsitter and international gnome thief, signing off.

Chris Pascoe's Fun Tales

CUP FINAL CALAMITY

How did a football team with hapless Chris in it ever reach the cup final? Well...

I was thinking the other day about political correctness and how things have changed since my school days, compared to the somewhat kinder way my daughter's generation are treated.

Regular readers may recall that I was a member of my school football team, by virtue of a few first-teamers deciding I "might be a bit of a laugh" rather than for any footballing skills.

Well, that football team once reached a County Cup Final. As my centre forward position in the team meant it was my job to score lots of goals, and I didn't actually ever score any, this in itself was a miracle, owing much to fate in the form of byes and broken down opposition buses.

On the day of the final, a lavish event attended by many county dignitaries, I can remember our trainer eyeing the opposition players for quite some time, before turning to take one short look at our team and appearing to come very close to tears. If he believed we had no hope and were definitely going to get beaten, we spectacularly exceeded all his expectations – we weren't just beaten, we were totally hammered to the point of annihilation.

To give some indication of the extent of this beating, midway through the first half, the referee briefly left the field, looking for a volunteer to record the score as he was finding it difficult to keep up. Sometime near the end of the match, I watched our trainer →

Nowadays we would probably have been offered counselling sessions

slipping quietly into his car and driving off (by this stage I was more interested in the car park than the football match).

So, in modern day Britain, I'm fairly sure I know exactly what would have happened to our team the next day at school. We'd have been told that taking part was what mattered, that there are no losers in sport (only non-winners), and that despite being totally thrashed, we'd all done extremely well. We would probably have also been offered counselling sessions, in the event of Post Traumatic Stress Disorder.

None of this was applicable in the early 1980s. On Monday morning, during our regular whole-school assembly, the Headmaster made an unexpected appearance.

School assemblies were always, absolutely always, run by deputy staff, and the Headmaster was rarely seen anywhere around the school, never mind in assembly. Indeed, his office was seen as sinister, a dark foreboding place that pupils quickened their pace to rush speedily by, and where nobody ever went unless they were in serious trouble.

The Headmaster strode onto the stage, raising a hand to silence the Deputy Head who was midway through his Monday monologue, and turned to face the surprised throng.

"Will all members of the school football team who took part in Saturday's Cup Final, please stand up," he boomed.

In various places around the hall, thirteen boys stood up. Our fellow pupils looked up at us in awe. "You are a disgrace to the school. Sit down," he said, and with that, left the stage.

Chris Pascoe's Fun Tales

AN UNLIKELY DOWNPOUR

It seems Chris isn't the only hapless chap – he can always blame his genes...

If there were ever any doubts that I'm my father's son, we've managed to dispel them over the past week. Our joint ability to turn normal everyday situations into personal credibility disasters was proven in two separate, but equally silly, situations.

First up was Dad, in a very unfortunate case of mistaken identity. I'd asked one of my catsitting clients, Colin, to put his front door key in an envelope and pop it through my parents' letterbox prior to his forthcoming holiday. The problems started when Dad spotted Colin walking up his drive and immediately mistook him for his former next-door-neighbour, who had left the area some years back and, not surprisingly considering his neighbours, had never been seen since. Dad rushed to the door to greet him only to see the envelope appearing slowly through the letterbox.

Astounded that he was just going to post something and leave without saying hello, Dad grabbed the envelope and hauled it through the letterbox with Colin's hand still attached, before swinging the door wide open and causing Colin to stagger forwards, throwing his arms around Dad in an effort to stay upright.

Dad took this to be a "long lost neighbour" hug and, returning the hug, happily blurted out, "You didn't think you were getting away that easily, did you?" I should think Colin was very happy to get away at all after that. →

GARDEN
WASTE

Meanwhile, I was keeping up my part of the family tradition down at the local rubbish tip. Where else would I be? I don't know what it is about the place, but the presence of so many tough looking skip attendants in hi-viz clothing and hard hats makes me feel I should act extremely cool and "salt of the earth" in an attempt to fit in. So I speak gruffly in a Mockney accent and try to do everything nonchalantly.

"Grass cuttings, mate?" I grunted to a huge shaven-headed tattooed attendant leaning on a skip. Without looking up he motioned a thumb over his shoulder at the very skip he was leaning on. I manfully swung my big bin bag of grass in the direction of the skip. Never buy cheap bin bags – anyone who says graphite is the thinnest substance known to man hasn't tried our local discount store's bin bags. The bag split mid-swing and a deluge of grass cuttings engulfed the skinhead sitting on the skip.

There were many tough looking skip attendants in high-viz clothing and hard hats

He was very good about it given the circumstances – and I even learnt new swearwords!

Talking of father's sons, try to work this riddle out... Imagine I'm looking at a family photo and pointing at one particular person, and I say, "Brothers and sisters have I none, but this man's father is my father's son." Which family member am I pointing at?

The puzzle has been in our family for generations and we've still yet to satisfactorily agree on the answer. OK, that may say more about our family than the riddle.

There are moments I think I have it solved, but then think... wait, no.

Chris Pascoe's Fun Tales

I DREAM OF WOMBLES!

It turns out that Chris's whole family has quite a lively nocturnal life...

I dreamed the other night that I was being attacked by a giant Womble. The possibility of this ever happening to me had never before crossed my mind. While the dream probably says quite a lot about my overall psyche, it also started quite a lively conversation at a family get-together at ours last weekend.

My mum was first off, complaining how Dad frequently wakes her in the night to discuss his dreams. This was news to Dad, who firmly believes he always sleeps through the night like a stone, even though he's up about 15 times and spends as much time in the toilet as he does in bed.

On this occasion, he had shaken Mum awake with the words, "I just dreamed I tried to blow up a caravan."

"Oh well, that's not too bad," replied a bleary eyed Mum. "I imagine that's quite a common dream." Blowing up a caravan is a common dream?

"No, it wasn't just that," he protested. "You were inside the caravan while I was trying to blow it up!"

"Oh," replied Mum, now fully awake. "Well, that's worrying." As Dad rolled over and settled back down he sleepily muttered, "No, it's OK. I haven't got a caravan." I feel he was surely missing the whole point of Mum's concern there.

While we were having this conversation, our cat Bodmin, who →

W

was out for the count on the sofa, joined in by suddenly growling in his sleep, baring his dagger-like claws, and ripping a hole in a nearby cushion, clearly dreaming about his favourite hobby, murdering things.

A collective shudder went round the room as we tried to ignore him – assisted in distraction by a loud thud from the utility room that had my wife racing to check the rabbits were OK. They were. Ted the rabbit, it appeared, had fallen asleep standing up, and simply keeled over sideways, making a sound like someone thumping a bass drum. You may think Ted was participating in the whole sleep theme going on, but he does things like that so regularly it doesn't count.

All this talk took me back to my childhood days when my sister and I both had a habit of sleepwalking. My own sleepwalking was fairly harmless – I'd get up in the night, firmly believing I was

The possibility of being attacked by a giant Womble had never crossed my mind

Captain Kirk. As my dad led me back to my bed, I'd complain bitterly, still fast asleep, and make repeated attempts to escape his clutches with shouts of "Beam me up, Scotty!"

OK, very odd I admit, but harmless nevertheless. My sister's sleepwalking on the other hand, wasn't quite so innocuous. Night after night, she'd get up in the early hours of the morning and walk into my room, before pouring the entire contents of the dirty laundry basket over my head.

When I told this story, my sister seemed quite taken aback. After frowning for a moment, she finally said, "Sleepwalking? Why did you think I was asleep?"

I'd always just assumed...

Chris Pascoe's Fun Tales

VIRTUAL UNREALITY

After four reboots, Chris's grasp on the real world has loosened considerably

I went to a theme park recently, probably through a niggling feeling I hadn't been suffering enough lately and needed a top-up. After doing the standard theme park thing of queuing two hours for a 10 minute thrill, we finally boarded a popular ghostly virtual-reality ride, to the recorded words, "You'll question what you saw on this ride."

Well, with me it went quite a bit further than that – I ended up questioning what I saw in the toilets afterwards. That's quite a disturbing sentence isn't it? I think I'd better explain myself.

Upon taking our coveted seats, we donned virtual-reality headsets, and I was absolutely stunned by just how very real everything seemed – I was immediately engulfed in another world, disturbingly like my own but with subtle differences, containing people and things that weren't actually there.

As is my luck with theme parks, things didn't quite go to plan. The ride broke down half way through, so they restarted it. Then it broke down again and, not wanting to let us down, they restarted it again. And again, and again, finally completing the ride at the fifth attempt. Consequently, after never having experienced virtual reality in my life, I spent an hour totally immersed in it.

By the time I staggered out of the exit, whatever part of my brain deals with distinguishing fact from fiction had gone on strike. →

My first stop was a nearby toilet, which was empty and dimly lit, looking eerily similar to scenes from the twilight world I'd just been experiencing.

As I stood washing my hands, an old man walked slowly into the room. It's a hazy memory, but I'm fairly sure I didn't think he was real. It's a measure of just how scrambled my senses were that, when he then turned to me and mentioned what a nice day it was, I jumped out of my skin, shouted in surprise and splashed him with tap-water. I then legged it out at breakneck speed, bouncing off both door frames as I went.

Fifteen minutes later, as I finally began to regain my senses, I told my wife Lorraine (who'd also been through the whole

I was absolutely stunned – I was immediately engulfed in another world

experience with no ill effects whatsoever) about the incident in the toilet. She looked confused. "I was standing outside the door... there was no old man... nobody went in after you."

To say a shiver ran down my spine is an understatement, but it wasn't nearly as bad as the shock I got a little while later when I idly looked over my shoulder to find the very same man a few feet behind me. My visible terror and muffled girlie scream came as a further surprise to him. "Are you all right son?" he said, looking genuinely concerned. "You seem a bit jumpy?"

So, thankfully, I was able to apologise and explain. All was well. However, Lorraine has yet to apologise for pretending "for a laugh" that nobody followed me into the toilets.

She's a cruel woman is Lorraine.

MISSING IN ACTION

Not one, but both of Chris's parents appear to have vanished...

I arrived at my parents' house yesterday to find it impersonating the Marie Celeste. The Marie Celeste, of course, was a ship famously found adrift on the ocean, completely devoid of crew. There were no signs of a struggle or stormy weather and there were unfinished meals on the ship's dining table. But the ship was completely empty. It remains one of the great maritime mysteries, and while my parents' house didn't quite aspire to those levels, there were eerie similarities.

Firstly, the front door was wide open, but no one was to be seen. Radio 2 played quietly in the background; Ken Bruce broadcasting to an empty house. Suddenly Alexa, the Amazon AI home assistant, gave a short beep and announced, "Here's your reminder – pick up my ass". OK, that was odd, but, given my parents' total inability to control Alexa, not altogether surprising. I listened as she repeated her reminder, just to check I hadn't misheard. I hadn't.

I looked out of the window into the back garden – no sign of life. I touched the kettle – recently boiled, but no hot drinks anywhere. I headed upstairs and looked around all the silent rooms. Baffling... they'd boiled the kettle, then gone out, the front door wide open, and left Alexa repeating a disturbing reminder.

As I checked the last empty bedroom, I got quite a surprise – there, at the window, was my dad, standing on an adjoining roof →

CHRIS !

and waving frantically at me. Rushing downstairs, I ran into the garden.

"Chris!" he yelled. "My ladder fell over! I've been stuck up here quarter of an hour." I noticed there was a cup of coffee up there, so two out of three mysteries solved. But what about Alexa's reminder? "Where's Mum?" I asked as I repositioned his ladder.

"She's gone to pick up Maya's birthday present." Aha, things suddenly made sense – Mum had slightly mispronounced her message and only managed to record half of it. Nothing mysterious there, then. In truth, I'm no better when it comes to dealing with

Given my parents' total inability to control Alexa it was not altogether surprising

our own Alexa at home. Last week my daughter Maya (whose present is now in Mum's custody) arrived home to find me in a heated exchange with Alexa.

Maya stood watching for a few moments before finally shouting, "OK, Dad – Alexa asked you for a simple 'yes or no' answer… and you answered 'Kung Fu Panda'."

"Yes, but that was the answer!" I blurted out. She stared at me in disbelief. "Alexa said to you, 'Do you want to quit? You replied, 'Kung Fu Panda'. How is that the right answer?"

OK, I'll admit it sounds a bit crazy when put like that, but I'd actually been playing a movie quiz, when things started to go wrong – I won't go into details, but I was still trying to answer a previous question. If Alexa ever turns against humanity, I bet my family will be number one on her revenge list.

ORDER FORM

CODE **MWPTB**

Please complete the coupon below and send it to: My Weekly Subscriptions, DC Thomson Shop, PO Box 766, Haywards Heath, RH16 9GF

YES, I would like to subscribe to **My Weekly** for:

❑ **BEST DEAL!** Only £7 for the first 3 months and £14 per quarter thereafter (UK) by direct debit*

❑ 1 year for £63.00 (UK) or £98.10 (Overseas) by cheque or credit/debit card

❑ 2 years for £119.70 (UK) or £186.39 (Overseas) by cheque or credit/debit card

Your Details

Title .... Name.. Address ....

....Postcode ....

Telephone..Email ....

Delivery Details (If different from above)

Title .... Name.. Address ....

....Postcode ....

Telephone..

DIRECT DEBIT

DIRECT Debit

INSTRUCTIONS TO YOUR BANK/BUILDING SOCIETY TO PAY BY DIRECT DEBIT

Originator's Identification Number

3 8 8 5 5 2

Name and full postal address of your Bank or Building Society

To the Manager	Bank/Building Society
Address	
	Postcode

Instruction to your Bank or Building Society
Please pay DC Thomson & Co Ltd Direct debit from the account detailed in this instruction subject to the safeguards assured by the Direct Debit Guarantee. I understand that this instruction may remain with DC Thomson & Co Ltd and if so, details will be passed electronically to my Bank/Building society.

Signature(s)

Name(s) of A/c Holder(s)

Date

Bank/Building Account No

FOR DC THOMSON & CO LTD OFFICIAL USE ONLY
This is not part of the instruction to your Bank or Building society.

Branch Sort Code

Bank and Building Societies may not accept Direct Debits for some types of account

DC Thomson & Co. Ltd and its group companies would like to contact you about new products, services and offers we think may be of interest to you. If you'd like to hear from us by post, please tick here telephone, please tick here or email, please tick here .
From time to time, carefully chosen partner businesses would like to contact you with relevant offers. If you'd like to hear from partner businesses for this purpose please tick here .